THE
GRINNING
KILLER

THE
GRINNING
KILLER

CHRIS HALLIWELL

**'HOW MANY WOMEN DO YOU HAVE
TO KILL TO BE A SERIAL KILLER?'**

NIGEL CAWTHORNE

JOHN BLAKE

Published by John Blake Publishing,
2.25 The Plaza,
535 Kings Road,
Chelsea Harbour,
London SW10 0SZ

www.johnblakebooks.com

www.facebook.com/johnblakebooks ❤
twitter.com/jblakebooks ❤

First published in paperback in 2018

ISBN: 978-1-78606-826-2

British Library Cataloguing-in-Publication Data:

A catalogue record for this book is available from the British Library.

Design by www.envydesign.co.uk

Printed and bound in Great Britain by Clays Ltd, Elcograf S.p.A

1 3 5 7 9 10 8 6 4 2

Text copyright © Nigel Cawthorne 2018

The right of Nigel Cawthorne to be identified as the author of this
work has been asserted by him in accordance with the Copyright,
Designs and Patents Act 1988.

Papers used b⟨…⟩ John Blake Publishing are natural ⟨…⟩ made from
wood grown ⟨…⟩ sustainable forest. The manufacturing pr⟨…⟩ m to the
⟨…⟩ the ⟨…⟩ country ⟨…⟩

Every att⟨…⟩ has been made ⟨…⟩ lders,
but some w⟨…⟩ ⟨…⟩ people

Jol⟨…⟩

CONTENTS

INTRODUCTION

In court in September 2016, as he was convicted of a second murder, Christopher Halliwell grinned at the families of the two women he had killed. Although he had confessed to it five years earlier, his confession of the second couldn't be used in evidence in court at that time as he was denied legal advice and not told that he had the right to remain silent. When he was eventually brought to book, he put the family of his second victim through the ordeal of a trial by pleading not guilty. Even though he'd led the police to the body, he later said the confession was false and he had only given it to get the policeman who interviewed him into trouble. Indeed, it ultimately led the detective to resign.

Halliwell, sentenced to a minimum of twenty-five years for the murder of Sian O' Callaghan and to life for the murder of Becky Godden, joins the select circle of prisoners who are serving a 'whole life' tariff. These included Moors Murderer Ian Brady; Yorkshire Ripper Peter Sutcliffe; Dennis Nilsen, who

THE GRINNING KILLER

clogged the drains in Muswell Hill with the boiled remains of his victims; Jeremy Bamber, who murdered five members of his adoptive family; Rosemary West of House of Horrors fame; Suffolk Strangler Steve Wright; Bus-Stop Stalker Levi Bellfield; paedophile Mark Bridger, who killed April Jones; Michael Adebolajo, one of the killers of drummer Lee Rigby; and most recently, gay serial killer and rapist Stephen Port. Halliwell, like the rest of them, will never get out.

Since his conviction for two murders, he has said nothing – but has he killed more and if so how many times? The cop whose career he ruined believes there is more to uncover. Police forces around the country are still investigating.

CHAPTER ONE

MY GIRLFRIEND IS MISSING

At 2.52 a.m. on the night of 19 March 2011, twenty-two-year-old office worker Sian O'Callaghan left Suju, a Japanese-themed nightclub in Swindon Old Town, to walk the half-mile home to the flat she shared with her boyfriend, Kevin Reape, a twenty-five-year-old quantity surveyor. She had only recently moved in with him and was still shifting her belongings from her family home to Kevin's.

There was some confusion about what her plans were that night. She disappeared without telling the two female friends she had been clubbing with that she was leaving. Her close friend, twenty-six-year-old Kate McLeod, said: 'When we were in the toilets in Suju she was outside speaking to this girl and she said, "I'll see in you in ten or fifteen minutes on the dance floor."'

On their 'girly night out', they had been for dinner and visited three nightclubs. Sian was clearly tipsy and perhaps her homing instinct had switched on.

THE GRINNING KILLER

At first, her friends thought she might have gone home because she was eager to get back to her boyfriend. Although they'd been going out for a couple of years, they had only decided to set up home together earlier that year. He was expecting her home, too, and sent her a text, saying simply: 'Worried x.'

The couple had exchanged regular texts throughout the day, each sealed with a kiss. The last message Sian sent was from Suju at 1.15 a.m. It read: 'Where are you x.' Kevin had been at the Cheltenham races that day. He did not respond immediately as he was asleep. He had gone to bed at about 10.30 p.m. as he was playing football the next day. When he awoke at 3.24 a.m., he texted her, saying: 'In bed, you?'

Sian didn't reply to his message, so he texted her friends asking if they knew where Sian was as she hadn't come home.

'We were waiting for her on the dance floor,' said Kate. 'We were in the club until half three looking for her. It was so out of character for her not to go home.'

Although Suju is not a big place, it had three rooms, each with its own DJ. The club had opened in an old town house in 2006. Friday nights were 'Electric Social', so the main room was playing UK garage, house, grime, and drum and bass, while the lounge played R&B and urban. It was open until 5 a.m.

Another friend, twenty-two-year-old Melissa Newman, said: 'Sian's such a sociable girl. She's lively and bubbly and loves going out with friends. She's the life and soul. She'd never just disappear.'

Sian was a PA for a company director in Swindon. A white girl, she was five feet three inches tall, of medium build, and had green eyes and brown hair cut in an asymmetric style. At least, that's the description the police gave of her later. That night she was wearing a grey dress, black bolero-style jacket, dark tights and flat boots, and was carrying a dark handbag with a beige flower attached.

The police in Swindon had already warned late-night revellers not to walk home following a series of sex attacks on women. Sian herself had been a victim of violence in Suju. On a previous visit, she'd been in the toilets when another woman punched her.

The night she went missing she was seen on CCTV walking out of the club on her own, past a small group of men. She then walked along the High Street in Old Town towards the flat she shared with Kevin in Westmorland Road. Although it was late, there were still a number of cars passing.

Kevin called both Sian's parents, who had separated, and contract her friends in case she had stayed with them. During that a fretful night, he kept trying to call and text but got no reply. Then, at 9.45 the following morning, when the battery of Sian's mobile phone ran out, he called the police and reported his girlfriend missing.

Sian's mother Elaine was away in Warwickshire that weekend. In the morning, she received a panicky phone call from her eldest son Liam.

'He said Kevin was really worried because Sian didn't make it home the night before and wasn't answering her phone,' she recalled. 'Kevin had already phoned around hospitals and informed the police. At the time, I thought it was a bit of an overreaction and that she'd probably just crashed at a friend's house.'

But when Sian still had not turned up by lunchtime, Elaine began to feel fearful.

'When I returned home that afternoon, I found two uniformed police officers at my front door,' she said. 'They were asking if this was normal behaviour for Sian. Suddenly it felt like things were escalating really quickly.'

When darkness fell and there was still no word from Sian, the uniformed police officers were replaced by plain-clothes detectives.

'My mind was all over the place,' Elaine remembered. 'I remember lying in the dark, unable to sleep and just staring at the ceiling until the birds started singing.'

The next morning, Elaine's older sister Sharon arrived.

'I collapsed into Sharon's arms, crying,' she said. 'I knew wherever Sian had gone, it was against her will and she wouldn't return the same girl.'

By midday, the house was swarming with police and there were endless phone calls from family and friends who'd seen Sian on the news.

'That day I was hit with so many questions and bits of information, I didn't have time to sit there and cry. I had to keep going,' Elaine said. 'All the while, I had to stay strong for my young son Aiden, who was only ten at the time.'

CHAPTER TWO

THE SEARCH
FOR SIAN

The Wiltshire Police checked the phone records and traced the activity on Sian's mobile to Savernake Forest, a remote woodland some thirteen miles from the Suju nightclub and Sian's Swindon home. A mast there had picked up a signal when Kevin sent his final text. By the following night more than sixty officers were combing the woods that covered more than 4,500 acres. Savernake Forest already had a murderous reputation: it was where Michael Ryan began the Hungerford massacre in 1987, when sixteen people died in his killing spree.

In a statement, Chief Inspector Mike Jones said Sian's family had grave fears for her safety. 'For Sian not to return home after a night out and not make any contact with family or friends is not only unusual for her but is something that she has never done before,' he said. 'This behaviour is out of character for Sian and her family is understandably very concerned for her welfare. She is normally an avid Facebook user, but has not used her account since earlier in the day on Friday. Sian doesn't appear to have any reason in her personal life that would indicate she might want to leave the area. Sian's family are extremely worried about her and we are offering them our full support.'

The family were too distressed to speak about Sian's disappearance at that time. Chief Inspector Jones appealed to Sian to contact the police, adding: 'It is very important that anyone who knows of Sian's whereabouts, or of any reason for her to stay away, contacts us immediately. A number of officers are involved in the search and our enquiries are ongoing.'

Sian's friend Kate McLeod told the press: 'We all want her to come home.'

Her thoughts were with boyfriend Kevin Reape.

'He must be in bits, so many people have contacted him about Sian,' she said.

Melissa Newman said that she had been looking forward to meeting Sian in Swindon that night. They had been friends since moving next door to each other at the age of nine.

'I texted her on Saturday to make sure we were still on for it, but she didn't reply,' Melissa said. 'Then by lunchtime I heard she was missing. She would never just disappear. She would always text us to say she was going home or getting a taxi.'

Her family were frantic and described her disappearance as 'completely out of character'. Meanwhile, her friends put up posters in the Old Town area and close to her home, and began an internet campaign to help track her down. More than a thousand people had joined a Facebook group to help find her that day, as pals said they were praying she returned home safely. Others appealed for help on Twitter. Elly Styles, another friend, wrote: 'Everyone is so worried, please come home.'

That Monday, Kevin Reape fought back tears as he launched an appeal for information to help find her.

'I just want to say how very worried we are about Sian,' he told a packed press conference in a police station in Swindon. 'She has been missing now for over two days and it's not like her to not come home or contact any of us for such a long time. We all want to know where Sian is and we want her home safe and well.'

He then spoke touchingly about the woman he loved.

'Sian is a bubbly, lively person and is instantly liked by everyone she meets,' he said. 'She is very close to her family and has lots of friends. We'd like to thank all of the people who have shown us support and helped search for Sian. Their kind words and gestures have been a great help to us. Someone out there must have seen or known where she is and we just want them to come forward and contact the police. This is a terrible time for all of us and we are praying for Sian's safe return. If Sian is listening and doesn't want to contact us I beg her to at least ring the police.'

He also expressed his gratitude to the media.

'We are all really grateful for the media coverage, which we are sure is helping to spread the appeal, but after the conference today we would really like to be left alone to deal with this difficult situation,' he said. 'We all just want to know that she's OK.'

Also present at the press conference were members of the O'Callaghan family – parents fifty-one-year-old Mick and forty-eight-year-old Elaine, as well as Sian's younger sister, nineteen-year-old Lora, and her twenty-four-year-old brother Liam.

'Walking into the room, I was blinded by a wall of camera flashes,' Elaine recalled. 'Around sixty photographers, journalists and police were packed into the small space, with all eyes on us. It was suffocating.'

The family had decided to let Sian's boyfriend speak for them.

'I didn't want any speculation about Kevin being involved in Sian's disappearance,' Elaine explained.

Elaine held Kevin's arm as he said, through sobs: 'It is breaking our hearts not knowing where she is. It's not like her to not to come home or contact us for such a long time.'

Liam added: 'Sian means the world to us and we just want her to come home. 'If anyone has any information, please help the police and come forward.'

Detective Superintendent Steve Fulcher, who was leading the inquiry, said he wanted to hear from anyone who could explain how Sian's mobile phone came to be in Savernake just thirty-two minutes after leaving Suju – a journey that could only have been made that quickly by car. It would have taken twenty-five minutes to drive there, raising the possibility that she had been lured into a vehicle. The police feared that she had been abducted. It was a 'nightmare scenario'.

'My concern is to find Sian O'Callaghan as quickly as possible in order to ensure her safety in these circumstances,' he said. 'It is totally out of character. Sian is a lovely girl, a pretty, attractive girl in a happy relationship with a loving supportive family.'

Nothing was known of her movements after she left the

Suju nightclub about 2.52 a.m., he said. Neither police nor her friends and family had been able to make contact with her after that time.

'At 3.24 a.m. Sian's phone is in the area of the Savernake Forest, which is why we've had significant activity concentrated in that area,' said Detective Superintendent Fulcher. 'What I am keen to do is find witnesses who can give me any indication of people moving about, of vehicles about, both in the Old Town area of Swindon from the time she left Suju nightclub at 2.52 a.m. I am also appealing for witnesses to come forward who either saw vehicles or people in the Savernake Forest area between 3.15 a.m. and 4 a.m. on Saturday.'

Fulcher stressed that Kevin Reape was not a suspect in the investigation and was being treated as a witness.

'That isn't the avenue that I think is going to provide the answer,' Fulcher said. 'He is not a suspect. I am happy with the account he has given.'

Wiltshire Police confirmed that Miss O'Callaghan was assaulted in the toilets of the same nightclub in October 2008, when another woman punched her. A twenty-four-year-old woman admitted the assault, but could remember little about the incident. It occurred in the early hours as she was leaving the toilet with a friend, and Sian and her friend were at a mirror fixing their make-up.

The woman had made eye contact with Sian and asked her what she was looking at. She then grabbed Sian by the hair, forced her to the floor, punched her and banged her head against the tiling. During the attack Sian hit her head on the basin. The attacker returned to the loo two more times to renew the attack, even though Sian never attempted to fight back. On one occasion Sian was kicked on her breast. She was left with bruises and a cut below her eye and seems to have lost consciousness. The next thing she remembered is being in the bar after an ambulance had been called. The whole thing was caught on CCTV. After admitting the offence, the attacker left Swindon and moved to Cardiff. She was given a twelve-month community order for 250 hours' unpaid work and ordered to pay £100 compensation.

'We are aware of a previous assault, but we are focusing on the here and now,' said a spokeswoman for the police. 'It is not a focus of the investigation at the moment.'

Fulcher also mentioned the sex attacks in Swindon. But they had occurred the previous year and the police downplayed any links between them and Sian's disappearance.

'I've looked at all of those, and all the intelligence that we have, and I have certainly discounted it,' Fulcher said. 'It is not a primary line of inquiry.'

The police released CCTV showing Sian alone in the nightclub in the hope it would jog fellow clubbers' memories about what she had been doing and whether someone had been with her subsequently. The footage showed her walking downstairs and going round a corner into another room out of shot.

Other black-and-white footage showed her walk out of the club's steel door alone. There were a small group of men outside, who the police were keen to contact. The police also noted that the times shown on the CCTV were approximately six minutes slow and urged anyone who remembered seeing her to contact them.

In the road immediately outside Suju there were no cameras. However, officers seized footage from two cameras outside a bank and pub about forty yards away on her route home.

'CCTV is currently being checked,' said an officer. 'One line of inquiry is that Sian got into a vehicle in the moments after she left the club.'

There was a night-time taxi rank right outside the club where she could have been picked up by a rogue cabbie and police began questioning taxi drivers in the area.

An anonymous donor, thought to be a local businessman, offered a £20,000 reward to help find the missing woman. Details of the offer came as hundreds of volunteers joined a search. The police issued a new poster, with details of the reward, which was pinned up across the county by volunteers. It also warned people to be careful and not to go out walking alone.

The poster included a picture of Sian, a still from CCTV footage showing her leaving Suju and a picture of her silver mobile phone, an LG E900 Optimus 7, which was somewhere in Savernake Forest the night she disappeared.

The caption read: 'A £20,000 reward has been offered anonymously for information that leads directly to Sian being found. Please contact police immediately if you saw Sian, anyone with her, or any vehicles either after she left Suju or in or near beauty spots between Swindon and Savernake between 3 a.m. and 4 a.m. Any information, no matter how trivial it may seem, could be vital to police enquiries.'

A police chief likened the search of Savernake Forest to looking for a needle in a haystack. He asked those who wished to help that day to report in at the Postern Hill campsite on the main A346 Salisbury to Marlborough road from 10.30 a.m. They should only attend, he said, if they were physically fit, and they should not bring dogs or search alone. By then, more than 24,000 people had joined a Facebook group set up to spread news of the search.

'The use of social media can be a very positive outlet for information,' said Salisbury Chief Inspector Bob Edge. 'However, I am also aware that there are a number of stories circulating on the internet regarding connection with other possible incidents and users need to be mindful that the accuracy of such entries cannot be relied on.'

Coaches were laid on to carry volunteers out to the campsite, and the Salvation Army set up emergency catering facilities. The huge turnout caused a correspondent at the *Western Daily Press* to question how the police coped with the ID and CRB checks needed before taking on anyone and how they managed to handle the risk assessments required: 'Do they have to engage in such exercises in the same way that others, using volunteers, have to or are the police exempted from these procedures or do they consider themselves to be exempt anyway?' wrote Philip Binding of Winscombe, North Somerset.

On Tuesday, 22 March, around four hundred people, including many of Sian's friends, lined up at the campsite, where they were divided up into teams and issued with blue plastic forensic gloves. They then joined specialist police officers to comb the thick undergrowth of Savernake Forest. Some broke down in tears when officers warned them to prepare themselves as there was a chance they would find Sian's body. The Wiltshire Search and Rescue team's police dogs also joined the hunt, while helicopters hovered above.

Kevin Reape was there with his brother Anthony. They had been searching the area since Sunday. Members of Sian's family were also there, along with her close friend Emma Shewry, a twenty-five-year-old assistant bank manager. 'We're all very upset and just want to find her,' said Emma. 'I've known her a long time. She is a well-loved girl.'

Sian's twenty-two-year-old friend Charlotte Yeandel said: 'She'd never go off with another man. Sian and Kev had never been happier.'

Another of Sian's friends, twenty-six-year-old Rachel Ewart, said: 'We just needed to do something to help. It's far better we're here trying to help than at home worrying about what may or may not happen.'

Twenty-seven-year-old Maz Wakefield came to give her support despite being on crutches. She said: 'I'd just be sat at home if I wasn't here and you want to do everything you possibly can. I'm really surprised about how many have turned out to help, I just hope it can make the difference.'

Among others helping was nineteen-year-old Mikey Jack, who played Sunday-league football with Kevin Reape.

'A lot of people here don't really know Kevin or Sian but they just want to help any way they can,' he said. 'Kevin's a great lad and he doesn't deserve this and my thoughts are with him and his family. He's a strong lad and I think deep down he's hurting a lot.'

The army of helpers searched the undergrowth with sticks. Within two minutes, one of the volunteers found a mud-covered handbag half-buried in thick foliage. It looked nothing like the dark handbag with a beige flower on it that Sian had been carrying that night, but an officer took it back to the police control centre for examination anyway.

CHAPTER THREE

NARROWING
THE SEARCH

By 1 p.m., scores of friends, well-wishers and Good Samaritans had joined the hunt. Two fifty-seater coaches brought even more people and long queues of potential helpers formed. In fact, so many people turned out to help that by mid-afternoon the police asked for no more to come.

One of Sian's friends who stayed at the campsite when she was told she would not be needed was twenty-one-year-old Lauren Smart. 'Swindon is a small community, we are all connected by mutual friends or family somehow,' she said. 'When something as awful as this happens we all want to help. I would like to think they would help me in the same situation.'

Forty-eight-year-old Tony Dean said he would stay until police told him to go home. 'If it was my daughter or sister I would want people to do what they could to help,' he said. 'I can't imagine what Sian's family are going through. If I can do anything to help them I will.'

At least a hundred people went off on their own to hunt when they were turned away from the official search because there were not enough trained officers to supervise them.

Local people, many of whom who did not know Sian or Kevin, joined in the search. James McMurray, a twenty-year-old labourer from Swindon, explained: 'I just wanted to do my bit. Nobody deserves to go through that and I'm doing my bit for the community.'

His friend, twenty-two-year-old Nick Glover said: 'We've come to help as it's quite dreadful what's happening. We're just hoping we find her. We'll do anything to help the investigation. I didn't know Sian but I saw it on the news and I thought I would come and help and do what I can.'

Another volunteer was seventeen-year-old college student Tizanne Gregory. 'I came here today in the hope of finding Sian,' he said. 'I'm just hoping we can do anything to help her parents and it is horrible not knowing where she is.'

Forty-year-old searcher Ann Lewis said: 'I've two daughters. This is every parent's worst nightmare.'

Leading the search, Sergeant Warren Knight praised locals for their outstanding response as there was a huge area to search. The mast had a range of six-and-a-half miles, so there were over forty square miles to cover.

'We are still treating this as a missing person inquiry,' said Sergeant Knight. 'We are a small force and this is a massive piece of woodland. The public's help has been fantastic but we don't have enough officers to marshal them.'

Knight and his team divided the forest into five sectors and sent out seven officers with up to seventeen volunteers each. The search continued until nightfall. By then they had only completed searching two of the five sectors. Afterwards, worshippers at Sian's local church, St Barnabas's in Gorse Hill, held a candlelit vigil and prayed for her safe return. It was organised by the Reverend Mark Paris and Canon Alastair Stevenson. Two hundred people attended.

In a statement released through police, Sian's family thanked the hundreds of people who had turned out to scour the forest as they searched for her: 'We have been so touched by the support shown by the community that we wanted to express our thanks. The sheer numbers of people who have given up their time to help search for Sian and distribute appeal posters are overwhelming and we couldn't ask for better support from the public, police and media. We are aware of the reward that has been offered and are very grateful. We hope that this might help someone come forward with information to help the police find her. This is an extremely difficult time for us and we continue to hope and pray that our beautiful girl is found soon.'

By then the reward had been upped to £40,000.

Sian's grandmother Peggy Pearce added: 'She is a beautiful, lovely person, how would anyone want to hurt her? We are just so shocked about it all. I will be going to see her mother Elaine to give her my support; we all need to pull together to support each other. If anyone knows anything they must tell the police everything they know.'

Detective Superintendent Steve Fulcher, who was leading what was still only a missing-person inquiry, said: 'I'd like to thank the public and media for their ongoing support with our investigation. My teams are working tirelessly to find Sian and the community have been very helpful and understanding. We know that Sian had an LG E900 Optimus mobile phone with her on the night of her disappearance and I'd like to hear from anyone who finds a phone of this description.'

He also appealed to drivers in the area on the night Sian disappeared. The possibility that Sian may have been picked up by an unlicensed taxi was one of several lines of enquiry the police were following. They were also investigating a report on Facebook from another clubber that two 'dark-skinned' men with foreign accents tried to coax a twenty-eight-year-old woman into a car in Swindon on Saturday night.

'It was pretty scary and shook me up a bit but I didn't think much of it until Sian disappeared,' she said.

Another woman was reported on the website to have been targeted by a driver the previous morning. His van was said to have been red, like one allegedly seen near the forest. The police in Swindon appealed for help to find a man who assaulted a woman in the Manchester Road area on the morning of the 22nd. A twenty-year-old woman was walking along Elmina Road at 10 a.m. when she was gestured at by a middle-aged man passing by in a rusty red van.

'Fortunately she wasn't injured but was very shaken up,' said DI Jim Taylor. Police said they had 'absolutely no reason' to link it to the inquiry into Sian O'Callaghan's disappearance.

Investigations in Swindon focused around the nightclub and officers pored over CCTV footage from cameras near the venue.

'Sian left Suju and walked along the High Street in Old Town and there were a number of vehicles moving through the High Street between 2.55 a.m. to 3 a.m.,' Fulcher said. 'We would like to identify the people in those vehicles as possible witnesses. I'd also like to hear from anyone who saw any vehicles in or near beauty spots between Swindon and Savernake between 3 a.m. and 4 a.m. It is very important that people come forward as they may have vital information which will help us to find Sian.'

Fearing the worst, he issued a stark warning.

'I'd also like to take this opportunity to remind people to think about their personal safety and take basic measures such as always making sure someone knows where you are going and what time you will be home,' he said. 'Stay with friends and try not to walk alone.'

The police were also examining social network sites, including Facebook, used by Sian and her friends.

'The investigation is very wide reaching and the comments and information on all sites, including social networking, are being considered,' said a spokesman.

Meanwhile Sian's co-workers at storage firm Dexion expressed shock and sadness at her disappearance. Operations manager Liz Watson said: 'We are all very worried about her at the moment and hope that further developments of her whereabouts will come to light soon. She is a well-liked and popular member of our team. Our staff are feeling very helpless at the moment. Our thoughts are very much with Sian's family and friends.'

Staff were in a state of shock and disbelief.

'Sian was always smiling,' said Watson. 'She attended work on Friday and was in her usual good spirits and looking forward to the weekend.'

By Wednesday the 23rd, the search area had been narrowed. Telephone experts mapped the huge area and ruled out sites such as valleys, where phones would not receive signals.

They had pinpointed hotspots and areas of interest where specialist officers were searching. Chief Superintendent Steve Hedley thanked the public for their help but said his force no longer needed support because the search area was now 'significantly smaller'.

'The telephone company has looked at the lay of the land and told us which parts of the area her phone could have received transmissions from and which parts it couldn't,' he said. 'We're still looking at a wide area but it's considerably narrower than before. Specially trained officers have now gone into these areas. We thank the public for their help so far. We have decided not to use them today but that doesn't mean we won't need them later in the week.'

Fulcher was confident that they would find Sian within a day. 'We have made good progress in narrowing the search using a number of technologies and techniques and I believe we are getting very close to identifying Sian's whereabouts,' he said. 'The inquiry moves on at a rapid pace, with significant lines of inquiry being developed. Searches will be limited by available daylight, but we will be further assisted by specialist dog teams who arrive tomorrow, and resume the search effort as soon as daylight permits. We are at a vital stage of the inquiry and I am optimistic we will have key developments within the next twelve to twenty-four hours. Whilst I still want anyone with information to contact police I am not asking for any more public assistance with searches at this stage.'

He added: 'I still hope she will be alive.'

Three detectives who worked on the case of missing twenty-five-year-old landscape architect Joanna Yeates also joined the investigation. She had gone missing in Bristol the previous December after an evening out with colleagues. The murder inquiry, codenamed Operation Braid, was one of the largest police investigations ever undertaken in the Bristol area. Her body was found in Failand, North Somerset, on Christmas Day and the case dominated news coverage over the holiday period. Although ultimately shown to have had no involvement, her landlord, Christopher Jefferies, who lived in a flat in the same building, was arrested. The guilty man was her thirty-two-year-old neighbour Vincent Tabak, a Dutch engineer. The police apologised for not making it clear sooner that Jefferies was innocent. Meanwhile, he had been vilified in the press. He sued eight publications for libel and won considerable damages.

Cold-case officers investigating the murder of twenty-five-year-old Melanie Hall, a graduate hospital clerical officer last seen alive in Cadillacs nightclub in nearby Bath in 1996, were investigating whether there were any similarities between the two cases. Avon and Somerset detectives had reopened the unsolved case in October 2009 when Melanie's badly decomposed body bound by a blue rope was found dumped by the side of the M5 at Falfield near Thornbury, about forty miles from Swindon.

The search in Savernake Forest was still drawing a blank when police revealed that they were looking for specific items.

'We are now appealing for information regarding items Sian is believed to have had in her handbag,' a spokesman said. 'Her handbag is described as a large dark-coloured bag with a beige flower on the side.'

The contents of the bag included a distinctively patterned front-door key, a black car key with yellow insulation tape, a Tesco Clubcard key fob, a yellow Kinder egg whose plastic casing contained an orangey-brown squirrel with a felt belly, and lip gloss. Sian was also thought to have been wearing or had with her a DKNY watch with fake diamonds and had been wearing a pair of brown boots.

By then, though, the police had their first real clue.

'I am urgently appealing for any witness sightings of a green Toyota Avensis estate with taxi markings seen between 3 a.m., 4 a.m. and 12 p.m. to 9 p.m. on Saturday, 19 March between Swindon and Savernake,' Detective Superintendent Fulcher announced. The hunt was now on.

CHAPTER FOUR

THE GREEN
AVENSIS

After Detective Superintendent Fulcher's appeal things began to move very fast. Examining the CCTV footage from the street outside Suju, the police had spotted Sian getting into a green Avensis after she left the club. It was also spotted circling the town. Number-plate recognition software had told them who it belonged to and, on Wednesday, 23 March 2011, the family were told that the police had a suspect under surveillance.

'As everything was unfolding in real life, it was on TV at the same time – it was surreal seeing Sian's face everywhere,' said Elaine. 'That day felt different, though. The family liaison kept rushing in and out of the house to take phone calls. There was so much going on, I knew something was about to happen. But then everything went silent.'

Fulcher had a dilemma as he paced the incident room. Should he pick the suspect up for questioning or should he leave him at large in the hope that he would lead them to Sian? But his hand was forced when the green Toyota estate was spotted at the taxi rank outside the Asda supermarket at the Orbital shopping centre in Haydon Wick, north Swindon. A police poster appealing for help in finding Sian was stuck in the back window. The driver was seen in the chemists buying a large amount – possibly a lethal dose – of paracetamol.

The police swooped at 11 a.m. Eight police cars raced to the scene and twelve officers arrested a thin white man, aged between forty and fifty.

'There were more than eight police cars surrounding a green taxi. The driver was white, short and very slim,' said a women shopper. 'They got him out of the car and hurriedly put him into an undercover police car. There was no delay or chat. They took him away straight away. A recovery truck came soon after and towed the vehicle away. As soon as I saw it, I knew what was happening.'

Another passer-by said: 'The arrested man looked terrified and was stammering with fear.'

Eighteen-year-old student Morgan Soble-Rees was taking his driving test when he saw the drama. 'The police cars suddenly appeared and blocked in a cab,' he said. 'The driver was short and very slim. They got him out of the car and quickly put him into an unmarked police car. There was no delay or chat. They took him away straight away. A recovery truck came soon after and took his taxi away.'

Twenty-four-year-old mother-of-one Tanya Fisher said her grandmother had called for the taxi. 'It sickened me when I realised it was the taxi the police wanted, as I saw he had put two posters with Sian's picture in the back window,' she said.

As the driver was handcuffed and bundled into the back of

an unmarked police car, he asked: 'How did you catch me? Was it the gamekeeper?'

Another witness, eighteen-year-old Zachary Ockwell, said: 'They dragged this man out and walked him over to the car next to me and stuck him in the back. They were not being gentle with him and were not polite. One of the officers said, "How would you feel if that was your daughter? How would you feel, mate?" The guy was shaking like a leaf and was really bricking it. He asked if he could smoke and pulled out a small black cigar and lit up and puffed furiously. The police were firing questions at him and asking him what he had done. He was puffing on his cigar like a chimney and was just a gibbering wreck. Other police officers put on blue gloves and started searching the car. Then a low-loader came and the taxi was loaded on board and driven off.'

An arresting officer said: 'He was shaking like a leaf. There were packets of tablets stuffed in almost all his pockets.'

The suspect had bought easily enough to overdose. Fulcher had made the announcement that the police were looking for a green Toyota Avensis to put the pressure on in the hope the rattled cabbie would then lead the police to Sian. But this had been the result.

The Toyota, which bore the logo of FiveStar Taxis, was loaded onto a trailer. Within two hours, the police were sent to guard the offices of the cab firm at Pembroke House in an industrial estate north of Swindon town centre.

The driver's house, a £180,000 three-bedroom end-of-terrace semi in Ashbury Avenue, on a 1960s housing estate in the Nythe area of Swindon, was searched. A white police tent was erected on the gravel driveway of the house, which was cordoned off with five policemen guarding it. Officers were seen digging in the garden throughout the day and items ere brought out to the three police vans parked outside. In all, the police took away ten bags of evidence, including two garden spades and some clothing. Later they were seen taking metal detectors and other machinery into the back garden.

Chief Superintendent Steve Hedley then made a public announcement: 'A short time ago a man was arrested on suspicion of the kidnap of Sian O'Callaghan and is en route to a police custody centre. Sian's family have been informed. It is a significant stage in this difficult inquiry. Our priority is to find Sian and we are doing all that we can to do so. Further information will be released in due course but it is not appropriate for me to make any further comment at this time.'

Asked if he thought the missing woman was still alive, he replied: 'We hope she is alive. We are certainly working on finding her and recovering her.'

And he cautioned the press.

But the police soon had the bad news and the blow fell as the family were informed that Sian was dead.

'Some parts of that day are a blur, but I still remember exactly where the family liaison stood in the room when she told us the news – I can even recall what her hair was like,' said Elaine. 'When she said they'd found Sian, I thought the next words would be "and she's alive". I was willing them to come out of her mouth. But they didn't.

'I grabbed Liam and Lora and told them it was OK to cry now. It was like we'd been given permission to let go. Later, when everyone had left and I knew the family were asleep, I went downstairs and sobbed so hard I couldn't breathe.'

Detectives were searching an area close to the Uffington White Horse, a 374-foot ancient chalk figure carved in the hillside nine miles away in neighbouring Oxfordshire. Part of the road and the verge was sealed off and was being guarded by a number of police officers, while a second forensics tent went up in a ditch. A canopy was also erected on the roadside and a tarpaulin placed over nearby undergrowth. Then four white-suited crime-scene investigators carried out a fingertip search in a taped-off zone while two helicopters were seen circling overhead. The site was hidden away in a wooded area as the road dips into a small valley. In a field near the tent, six more uniformed officers scoured the ground.

Angus Tucker, landlord of the Blowing Stone pub in nearby Kingston Lisle, said that customers had told him a section of the B4507 was cordoned off. The stretch, which runs west to east from Broadway, south of Uffington, to Blowingstone Hill, south of Kingston Lisle, had been closed off that afternoon.

'Well, I know it's been cordoned off since 5 p.m., but it could well have been before that,' he said. 'I am told there are quite a few police.'

That evening, Fulcher held another press conference. He had a shocking announcement to make. Not only was Sian dead, but there had been another victim.

'A forty-seven-year-old man from Swindon is in custody, having been arrested for kidnap and two murders,' Fulcher said. 'The locations of two bodies have been identified to me by this individual, one of whom has yet to be identified formally, but I am quite clear is Sian. I have informed Sian's family, who are obviously deeply distressed, and I would ask you please to give them time and space to come to terms with what's happened. The public and the media have been a fantastic help in the desperate effort to find Sian over the last few days. This has, of course, been a fast-paced inquiry. Having found these bodies, you will appreciate that I am under extreme pressure to undertake certain actions and procedures, and I would ask you to give me some time to enable me to recover these bodies, with the dignity and respect that they deserve.'

He said he was concerned for the family and the effect this would have on them. Kevin was said to be inconsolable.

The police then issued a formal statement, saying: 'Wiltshire Police would like to make it clear that while the location of two bodies has been identified to the senior investigating officer, only one body has currently been found, and this is believed to be Sian O'Callaghan. The second body has yet to be recovered.'

The discovery of Sian's body came six days after she had gone missing. After a short search of the area, it had been found near the Uffington White Horse beauty spot. The police had still to find the second body of an, as yet, unidentified victim, though the suspect had divulged its exact location. Fulcher refused to give further details.

The man in custody was taxi driver Christopher Halliwell, a divorcee who lived with his partner Heather Widdowson, six years his senior, and her three young daughters. Two of his stepdaughters knew Sian.

Halliwell and his ex-wife Lisa, whom he had left eight years earlier, had three children of their own – Natasha, nineteen, Carissa, seventeen, and a twelve-year-old son – who were also friends with Sian.

'Chris knows Sian so she would have not had a second thought about getting into a car with him,' said a friend. 'He's a family man and seems a really nice bloke. He looks younger than he is and gets on well with people. Sian knows him through his kids as they go out together.'

It was later said that the police had kept him under surveillance for at least two days, that the police followed him to a wooded area the night before his arrest and were investigating whether he had disposed of any evidence.

Halliwell had often been seen tinkering with his Toyota outside the house. A neighbour, seventy-one-year-old retired toolmaker Brian Jerome, said: 'Chris is a smashing bloke. He is very funny. If it's raining outside he'll come out and say, "All right Brian, is it hot enough for you?" He works shifts, his work is staggered. He's a great guy. I can't believe it. I've all the admiration in the world for Chris. He's a devoted family man. I'm sure this will be a mistake.'

They had become next-door neighbours five years earlier.

'They are the sort of couple who you would choose to have as neighbours,' said Jerome. 'I'm in shock and I hope the police have got it wrong. Everyone in the area is shocked about this, I suppose things happen anywhere but you don't expect it on your street.'

Another neighbour said: 'It's crazy. I went to the chippy for lunch and came back to find officers in his garden. They have been picking up the shingle and paving stones on the drive.'

Halliwell had lots of different cars, but Jerome confirmed that he had had the green Avensis for a while.

His forty-five-year-old sister, Sarah Wrenn, who lived just twenty miles away in Stroud, had had nothing to do with him for decades. 'I have had hardly anything to do with him for twenty years,' she said. 'There wasn't really a big falling out. We just stopped communicating with each other. I haven't kept in touch with him because I don't want a bad influence in my life. He had no contact with my mother. And she didn't even ask about him when she died a couple of years ago. He couldn't sustain relationships with the family. But I can't see him doing anything like this and I hope he's not involved.'

But she admitted that he was the black sheep of the family.

'He's been in trouble a lot,' she said. 'He has always had a dark side.'

The household had other problems. Court records showed that Halliwell, who was described as a 'self-employed driver', was declared bankrupt the previous January. According to the petition at Swindon County Court, he had been 'carrying on business under the style of George's Chauffeur Services as a chauffeur'. He had been a cab driver in Swindon for ten years. For three years, he had driven for United Radio Cars, but switched to the newly established FiveStar Taxis a fortnight before his arrest.

'We only started up two weeks ago and he had just joined us, so I can't tell you too much about the guy,' said the cab firm's controller. 'He seemed decent enough, put in a lot of hours and would work until the early hours. We have just started up business and only have seven or eight drivers. He is the only one in a Toyota Avensis. If it turns out he did this then he deserves everything he gets.'

A cab driver who used to work with Halliwell said: 'He works the late shifts and is a regular on the nightclub runs. He's slim and has piercing blue eyes and I suppose women would find him quite attractive. I know him well and for him to be arrested is a huge shock.'

A friend regularly given lifts from nightclubs in Swindon by Halliwell said: 'I trusted him totally. I have given his phone number to at least five young women telling them to use him to get them home safe and sound. Thinking of what they say he has done makes my blood run cold.'

Before working for United Radio Cars, Halliwell had a contract with computer chip giants Intel Corporation – whose UK head office is in Swindon – to ferry senior staff to and from Heathrow Airport.

Ray French, whose company Chauffeur Driven Car Hire hired Halliwell, said Halliwell was recommended by other drivers.

'He was polite, reliable and hard-working. I would have trusted him with my own daughter,' said French. 'We hired him on a casual basis to assist with contracts we had with Intel, Nationwide, Honda, WH Smith and Zurich Assurance – all of whom have their UK head offices in Swindon.'

Just twenty-four hours before his arrest, Halliwell had joked to friends: 'They're looking for a green taxi – I wonder if they're after me.'

Fellow taxi driver and close friend Neil Barnett told the *Sunday Mirror*: 'I can't believe Chris was joking about the police being after him one day and was arrested the next. I've known him for ten years and he seemed completely normal. It is shocking he might have killed two people.'

Barnett had met Halliwell and two other friends at Swindon's Dockle Farmhouse pub for breakfast at 9.30 a.m. on Wednesday, four days after Sian had gone missing. By that stage, detectives were already watching Halliwell's movements.

'It is a cab drivers' get-together once a week,' said Barnett. 'That day there were three of us already there, then Chris arrived and ordered a full English. We must have stayed about an hour. We started talking about Sian – I saw Chris's taxi had an appeal poster in its window. At that stage they weren't looking for a taxi driver, so we didn't talk about where we were on that night. Chris said, "I can't believe that this has happened – this sort of thing is not supposed to happen in Swindon. I hope the police manage to catch whoever has done this." He also said he was worried for his own daughters' safety.

Even when Neil heard the taxi that police were looking for was a green Toyota Avensis, like the one Halliwell drove, he did not suspect his friend.

'I didn't begin to think it could be Chris until I heard he had been arrested,' said Barnett. 'It is incredible to think he's been driving young girls around this town for ten years and none of us thought he was remotely dangerous.'

Just hours before Halliwell was arrested, he allegedly told taxi boss Marion Spencer: 'You never know what you might find in the forest.'

A fellow taxi driver said: 'Marion didn't take much notice of what Chris had said until his arrest. They were sitting down having tea in the cab office when Chris just came out with it. They hadn't been talking about Sian. Marion just brushed it off at the time.'

But Halliwell's younger sister Sarah expressed no surprise.

'He has always had a dark, disturbing streak,' she said. 'It came to the surface when he was a little boy and may have again.' She added: 'If it is proved he has done these things they should lock him up and throw away the key.'

Their mother had split from their dad, who worked for the RAF, and went to live in Scotland with their stepdad. Halliwell had a troubled upbringing until he was finally flung out by his mother as a teenager. He knocked around the country working as window cleaner, builder, binman, chauffeur and taxi driver.

Eventually he settled in Swindon, where he met Lisa Byrne, a shop assistant, in the late 1980s. He was twenty-three; she was sixteen. They moved in together, married in the mid-1990s and had three children. They lived at a number of addresses in Swindon then moved into number 24, Ashbury Avenue in 2001. Five years later, he left Lisa and moved in with Heather Widdowson, six doors down the street in number 12.

His best mate, Aaron Body, said that Halliwell repeatedly cheated on Lisa with a string of lovers before he eventually moved in with Heather. 'He told me he had flings with another two or three girls when he was still with Lisa,' said Body. 'I don't know how he pulled them because he didn't have the greatest banter.'

He started paying for sex after his wife had their third child and was a regular user of prostitutes.

By the time he was arrested, both of Halliwell's parents were dead; his partner Heather left the country. Her brother Peter Spanswick said: 'She is in pieces and was barely even able to talk to me on the phone. She simply had no idea about any of this and would hate anyone to think she did.'

Detective Superintendent Fulcher revealed that the breakthrough in the case came from the green Avensis. CCTV established that it was near the club at the time Sian went missing. It had driven passed her, then come back, stopping next to her.

'CCTV images gave me an indication that the abduction of Sian was conducted by a individual driving a green Toyota

Avensis,' said Fulcher. 'Further analysis gave me the vehicle registration. I believed that it was likely that Sian had been abducted and taken away in this vehicle.'

Later the police gave the *News of the World* further details of the telltale footage that had led them to Halliwell.

'His car was spotted on the road outside the Suju nightclub on CCTV. We saw it turn round and drive back down. The problem we had was that at the moment he pulled close to Sian as she walked down the street, the beam of his car's lights dazzle the camera. We know that was the point of abduction but we can't actually see it. When we arrested Halliwell he was keen to stress that he had not sexually assaulted Sian and we have not found any evidence to show otherwise.'

Halliwell's taxi was spotted 'prowling' the streets of Swindon's Old Town on CCTV after he had officially signed off work at 2.13 a.m. Two minutes after Sian was seen getting into the car, an automatic number-plate recognition camera fitted to a police car recorded him leaving town in the direction of Savernake.

CHAPTER FIVE

THE SECOND VICTIM

According to a police source, Halliwell did not deny abduction and murder, and voluntarily led officers to where he said he had disposed of the bodies, though neither was found straight away.

'At first he was quite talkative and calm,' the informant told the *News of the World*. 'He was clearly a man who was contemplating what he had done and what it meant for the rest of his life. He claims to have killed both of the victims in different ways. When we were taken to the second spot, he pointed right at the very spot and we got an officer to stand there marking it while we returned with the search teams.'

Halliwell's modus operandi and motivation remained unclear.

'We have not quite worked out how she was killed but it was a brutal murder,' said the informant. 'We think that the fact that she was found naked is more to do with something in Halliwell's psychology.'

Earlier that day, activity had been seen at the Uffington. Shortly after 10 a.m., a convoy of police vehicles went through the cordon at the site where Sian's body had been found. The six- or seven-strong cavalcade included police cars and vans, along with an unmarked van towing a white trailer. A post-mortem examination was then underway, Fulcher said.

'This is a tragic situation, I have spoken to the family,' he added. 'Our thoughts are with Sian and her family.'

Sian's body was found quite easily. It had been dumped in the undergrowth. But according to Halliwell, the other victim had gone missing several years earlier and he had buried her. Fulcher said that there was only one outstanding missing person on the records of the Wiltshire Police.

'What I can say is that if there is one, it relates to an incident some years ago,' said Fulcher, but he would not be draw further at that point. 'I can tell you that Wiltshire only has one outstanding missing adult and that is from several years ago. It is not appropriate for me to reveal any detail.'

According to *The Guardian*, the only Wiltshire resident listed as missing on the missing persons website was a fifty-three-year-old man called Anthony Fryer, who vanished from Swindon in 2005. However, the *Western Daily Press* reckoned the second victim was thirty-nine-year-old mother-of-three Tina Pryer, who was last seen getting in a taxi in Trowbridge, Wiltshire, on Easter Sunday, 2001. Other names were soon in the frame.

There was speculation that the second victim was a prostitute who was said to have had personal problems and, at the time she disappeared, was thought to have left the area. Consequently, she was not listed as missing. Or it could have been forty-one-year-old teacher Linda Razzell, who had going missing a short drive from Suju in March 2002.

THE SECOND VICTIM

'I hope it is Linda's body, for everyone's sake,' said a friend. But Mrs Razzell's cousin, Julie Westmore, said she had 'no doubt' that the second body was someone else. Although Linda's body had never been found, Glyn Razzell, Linda's estranged husband, was convicted of her murder in 2003, though had always protested his innocence. Again, because of his conviction, Linda Razzell was not listed as a missing person as she was believed to be dead.

Detectives investigating the disappearance in 2007 of fifty-seven-year-old Kate Prout from her home, a farmhouse in the Forest of Dean in Gloucestershire, were also understood to have been in touch with Wiltshire Police. Then there was Laura Stacey, who had disappeared leaving the Destiny & Desire nightclub in Swindon on 20 January 2003, the papers said. Or perhaps it was Thi Hai Nguyen, a twenty-year-old Vietnamese woman who vanished from Swindon in 2005.

The police were said to be working on the theory that the second victim came from a different part of Britain, or had not been reported absent as Wiltshire Police have no missing persons on their books from the period when the crime was thought to have taken place. Perhaps no one knew she was in Swindon when she vanished. The charity Missing People pointed out that 250,000 people disappear in the UK every year.

If there were two victims, could there be more, the newspapers were soon asking.

Criminologist Dr Kate Painter of Cambridge University said: 'Men who are proven to have killed twice in a period of ten years have often killed again in between. Research shows a person normally does not start suddenly killing when they reach middle age.'

The press were soon asking whether Sian was the last victim of a serial killer; the police were investigating this possibility too. After Halliwell moved into number 24 with wife Lisa and the children, he had laid a large concrete patio. A close friend had offered to lend a hand.

'I knew he worked very late seven days a week in his taxi so offered to help him out,' said the friend, 'but he was adamant that he wanted to do it all on his own.'

In the history of crime, Fred West was not the only one to bury his victims under patios. The body of drug dealer Arthur 'Joe the Crow' Rouse was found under a patio in West London. The head of fifty-four-year-old Susan Craven was destined for the patio, said Kenneth Peatfield, her lover, who was convicted of her murder. The police found it encased in a two-foot concrete block. And a surprising number of bodies find themselves buried in the back garden.

After Halliwell left Lisa in 2006 and moved in with his new partner Heather Widdowson at number 12, he was digging again – this time, deep foundations for a conservatory. According to a friend: 'One of his best mates who has gone fishing with him for years offered to help him build it; he again said he was fine and wanted to do it on his own.'

Meanwhile, there were more solid leads. Following information given to them by the suspect, the police were searching a site first said to be outside Northleach, Gloucestershire, though it turned out to be nearer Eastleach, seven miles away. Efforts to find the second body were complicated by the fact that the field had been regularly ploughed.

'Searches of that area continued through the night. It is a painstaking and slow process,' said Fulcher. He frankly admitted: 'We do not at this stage know what we are dealing with.' However, claims that police were searching for a third body were dismissed.

The police were seeking more time to question Halliwell while they were still looking for the second body, so an application was made to the local magistrates to extend the suspect's detention. At the time, Halliwell was in police custody at Gablecross Police Station and he was driven to Swindon Magistrates' Court for a short hearing, travelling in a high-security van escorted by three police cars and a motorcycle outrider. He was bundled into the court – where he had once been a cleaner – under a blanket. A twenty-four-hour extension was granted, so he could be held in custody without charge until 3.15 a.m. on Monday. Then the police had to either charge or release him.

'He currently remains in custody here at Swindon,' said Fulcher. 'During the course of dealing with him I was personally taken to two locations. One near Uffington, where we discovered the body of a woman who we believe is Sian, and also to another location near Northleach, where I believe a second body may have been taken.'

During the trip, he said Halliwell had been handcuffed and videoed.

'I believe that Sian's body was moved to the Uffington area by this individual,' said Fulcher. 'Sian's family have been fully informed through the night, including the fact that Sian's body has now been recovered.'

He later confirmed that, as the media coverage and public hunt for her intensified, Halliwell had moved Sian's body from the spot where he had murdered her in Savernake Forest to the place where it was found, near the White Horse at

Uffington. He had returned to the scene of the crime under cover of darkness to perform his grim task.

Halliwell had led him to the spot where they found Sian's body lying in the undergrowth, Fulcher said. They had arrived at the second site on the Oxfordshire–Gloucestershire border at around 5 p.m. and Halliwell led him to a spot near a set of gateposts, just inside a field next to a crossroads, where the police were currently searching. It was in the rolling countryside a couple of miles south from the Cotswold Wildlife Park, outside the small market town of Burford.

Fulcher refused to discuss reports they had been in contact with police in Somerset regarding the 1996 disappearance of Melanie Hall. Avon and Somerset Police also refused to comment.

The police had set up roadblocks on five roads around the Gloucestershire villages of Eastleach Turville and Eastleach Martin, about ten miles north of Swindon, and scoured the area around Baxter's Farm, between Eastleach and Filkins, for clues. They were using mechanical diggers to excavate the corner of a field.

Village resident Julian Selby-Rickards said: 'This is such a sleepy backwater sort of place. There were police helicopters flying around but we thought nothing of it until we saw the roadblocks. It's desperately sad. I can only hope that if they do find someone, it will bring closure to their loved ones.'

A blue tent had been erected in the field and around fifteen officers and forensics experts were searching land. They had removed part of a drystone wall and excavated two trenches four feet deep in the corner of the field, removing tons of earth. Officers in protective clothing were seen on their hands and knees in the mud.

THE SECOND VICTIM

The field was owned by farmer Anthony Kinch, who said: 'That field has been ploughed so many times it will be hard to find anything there. All I can say is it is not far from the road, the area where they are looking.'

Graham Soule, whose property overlooked the search area, said a group of plain-clothed officers arrived at 3 p.m. on Thursday. Later, figures in white suits could be seen erecting a blue tent and the search ranged over a quarter of a mile.

Detective Chief Inspector Sean Memory, who was leading the search, said officers had received relatively specific information from a man held in connection with Sian's murder but after a day nothing had yet been found.

'We were given some indication of where there might be a find,' he said. 'Of course, it isn't as simple as that. It was tricky last night in the dark. We will use as much light as we can and then decide what we will do when it gets dark.'

They brought powerful floodlights and the search continued for a second night. Then, on Saturday, 26 March, the police found what they were looking for. Detective Superintendent Fulcher said: 'This morning officers have found remains which we believe to be human at the site at Eastleach.'

An official police statement confirmed the find.

'The remains that were found this morning are of a second body,' it said. 'We believe that they are bones from an arm or a leg and we are confident that they are human remains. It will take us at least six or so hours to ascertain the exact nature of the bones and we expect to recover further remains. If we can obtain orthodontic records and DNA we hope to know the identity of this person within the next forty-eight hours. We believe that they are of a young woman who disappeared from the Swindon area between 2003 and 2005, but there are no official records of any woman reported missing during this time. She may have come from outside of the Swindon area or her disappearance may just not have been reported at the time because she had no family or friends.'

Chief Superintendent Hedley cautioned the press: 'This has been a really difficult week and we must not forget that Sian's family are grieving and we know that at some stage another family who are missing their daughter will also be grieving.'

The police refused to speculate on the identity of the second set of remains for fear of causing undue distress or raising false hopes among relatives of missing people, saying only that site was seventeen miles from where Sian's body had been discovered.

Fulcher added: 'Bones recovered from the site at Eastleach in Gloucestershire are believed to be that of a young woman with an estimated age of between twenty-three and thirty years. It has been indicated to me that this young woman was taken from the Swindon area between 2003 and 2005. The remains will now be subject of further forensic laboratory tests and a post-mortem examination. The police search at the site is expected to continue for the time being.'

Fulcher confirmed that the information about the second victim had come from Halliwell.

'He couldn't be specific about the dates or the year, but he was able to give me the exact location of the body,' Fulcher said. 'He told me that a young woman had been taken by him from the Swindon area.'

The detective also appealed for anyone who had been poaching or 'lamping' – hunting rabbits using a bright light – in the Ramsbury area of Wiltshire or nearby after 3 a.m.

on Saturday, 19 March to contact the force if they had seen anything suspicious, or they had seen a green Toyota Avensis. Fulcher added: 'I want to stress that we only want information from you that is relevant to the Sian O'Callaghan inquiry. We are not interested in prosecuting anyone for lamping or poaching.'

By this time, Sian's body had been formally identified.

'Sian's body has since been successfully recovered and formal identification was carried out by Sian's family,' Fulcher said. 'A post-mortem has been done, but further tests are still required to determine the cause of death and this may take some time. At this time there is no indication that Sian was sexually assaulted. We believe the individual who murdered Sian also killed a young woman at some point between 2003 and 2005. We can't be specific about the date or the year but we were given the exact location of the body. The young woman had been taken from the Swindon area. Officers have begun work to recover this second body and this morning officers have found remains which we believe to be human. Work is ongoing at the site.'

The police were looking into the theory that the two alleged murders had been carried out with different motives. The first was thought to have happened around the time Halliwell's marriage was crumbling and may have been related to his mental state at the time. The second did not seem to be sparked by any specific event in Halliwell's life. It seemed to be opportunistic, though it appeared that Halliwell knew Sian through his partner's daughters and his own.

Halliwell's nineteen-year-old daughter Natasha posted on Twitter: 'My heart, and my families [sic], go out to all those affected by this especially Sian's family & any families with missing people awaiting news.'

This brought the response: 'Oh Tashy, you're so lovely. I'm thinking of you babe.'

A friend of Natasha's told the *Sun*: 'That's the kind of caring person Natasha is. Sian was a young girl going about her business when this awful murder happened in the home town they shared. Natasha feels her family's pain although they weren't close friends.'

Natasha also hinted that her own family life had been difficult. She said on Facebook: 'It's a shame we can't choose our families.'

A friend said that Natasha and her younger sister Carissa had been very protective of their mum, Lisa, since the divorce. The two girls had also been furious over a remark on a social-networking site about Sian when she had gone missing. It compared her to a cat 'stupidly waiting outside for a lift home at one to three in the morning'.

Carissa wrote: 'You're f****** sick. A girl has gone missing. No one knows if she's alive or not.' Natasha added: 'Whoever said that Sian "joke" is seriously f*****d up.'

With Halliwell now in custody, more came out about the events leading up to his arrest. He had been under surveillance from Tuesday until his arrest on Thursday. The police decided not to arrest him straight away in case he had merely kidnapped Sian and she was still alive somewhere.

'The feeling was that if Halliwell was arrested immediately he could deny everything and we would never find Sian,' a police source told *The Sun*. 'A decision was made to tap all his means of communication and monitor his movements to see whether he was spooked enough to return to the scene or to contact a possible accomplice. However, by Thursday morning, it was clear that he was continuing life as normal and nothing was to be achieved by allowing him free rein, so we sent in a team to bring him in.'

The night before the police arrested Halliwell, they watched him light a bonfire among the trees and burn unidentified items, but did not move in.

'The officers had to stand back and make sure they were not seen. But they were clearly suspicious and became very concerned when they saw a bonfire leap into life,' *The Sun* was told. 'All that remained afterwards was ashes. It led directly to the decision to arrest him the next day.'

The case was receiving huge publicity and, that Friday, the BBC pulled the fifth episode of the *Woman's Hour* drama 'Cottonopolis', because it was about a missing woman and a taxi driver who wrongly came under suspicion. This was a blow to the playwright Michelle Lipton, who had already written about how difficult the series was to write as its multiple storylines had to be pulled together in six episodes. The remainder of the series was postponed indefinitely.

Then, on Saturday afternoon, at the club where Sian played bowls, the team stood in silence out of respect, and the players at Swindon Town Football Club wore black armbands as a tribute to Sian at their away game at Brighton. They announced they would hold a minute's silence before the following week's home game against Hartlepool. Many of the players were regulars at Suju and wanted to express their condolences.

Former Swindon Town striker sixty-five-year-old Don Rogers said: 'It's brilliant from the club. Her death will have affected most fans.'

THE GRINNING KILLER

That evening, at 7.30, an estimated ten thousand people gathered in the Polo Ground in Swindon for another vigil. After two minutes' silence, they said the Lord's Prayer and released a thousand Chinese lanterns and balloons, many of them with personal notes on. In an outpouring of emotion, people lit candles in Sian's memory, started singing songs, shouted out their own tributes and comforted each other.

Veronica Cooper, a friend of the family, said: 'It's all such a shock – I can't believe it. All my family knew her. She was such a lovely, bubbly, kind person. It's such a horrible thought to think it could happen. I'm glad that she's at peace now.'

The event – called Lighting Up The Sky For Sian – was arranged via Facebook before her body was found and was intended to 'light the way home' for Sian, but tragically became her memorial. A message on the Facebook page read: 'We are, sadly, no longer lighting Sian's way home, we are lighting the sky to show that a life has been taken but will not be forgotten.'

Liz Williams came the seventy miles from Cirencester to take part.

'It was an honour to participate in something so moving,' she said. 'It was a beautiful sight to see and I am sure Sian would've loved every second of it.'

Later, an appeal was made for people to stop using Chinese lanterns in a letter published anonymously in the *Western Daily Press*. It said: 'On January 4, I picked up nine lanterns from our fields, thus preventing these wire-based objects being harvested as animal feed later in the summer, so the picture of 1,000 lanterns released is disappointing as this will put at risk many livestock and wildlife. Please no Chinese lanterns for any occasion and at the Polo Ground, candles would have been a lovely tribute.' The name and address of the correspondent was supplied, but withheld by the newspaper.

With the family's consent, the more than three hundred bunches of flowers, cards, candles, teddy bears and messages from Sian's friends and well-wishers lining the pavement outside the Suju nightclub were being moved from the doorway, as the club planned to re-open for the first time since Sian's disappearance. Tributes had piled up there. 'You were a great person and friend,' read one note. 'I knew you for 15 years since Drove Primary School and we stayed in touch since. Will remember your trademark big smile was lovely.' There was also a bouquet from Kevin Reape's family. The note with it read: 'Our sister-in-law. You will always have a place in our hearts.' The flowers were collected by the police. More flowers were laid near the spot where her body was found, with a message saying: 'Sian, All our memories and thoughts are of you. With love from all at Dorcan School.'

Elsewhere in the town centre of Swindon a street artist painted her name with an angel's wing attached on a wall in Cambria Bridge Road. Online there were other tributes to her beautiful, smiling nature. A former colleague wrote on the *Swindon Advertiser* website: 'It seems she always had a smile on her face. Such a beautiful girl. She'll be in our memories forever.'

Meanwhile, it was rumoured that members of Halliwell's family had received death threats. Louise Laveridge, one of those who had placed flowers in Sian's memory outside Suju, said: 'I have heard that the wife and kids are getting death threats. That's wrong.'

A police spokesman said that the force would not comment

on the accusations, but said: 'If she [his wife] has been receiving death threats we will be dealing with it appropriately.'

CHAPTER SIX

CHARGED

At 9.20 p.m. on 26 March 2011, Christopher John Halliwell, aged forty-seven, of Ashbury Avenue, Swindon, was charged by Wiltshire Police with the murder of Sian O'Callaghan. Simon Brenchley, Wiltshire District Crown Prosecutor, said: 'I have been working closely with Wiltshire Police and now have authorised them to charge Christopher Halliwell with Sian O'Callaghan's murder. Having reviewed the evidence, I am satisfied that there is sufficient to charge him, and that it is in the public interest to do so. I will keep liaising closely with the police as their investigation continues.'

Brenchley also issued a warning: 'I must remind the media to take care in reporting events surrounding this case. Mr Halliwell has been charged with a serious offence and is entitled to a fair trial. It is extremely important that nothing should be reported which could prejudice any trial. I will keep liaising closely with the police as their investigation continues.'

Halliwell remained in custody at Gablecross Police Station in Swindon where he was being questioned about the second victim. As yet, no charges had been made in respect of the second body, whose identity had still not been established. It was said that dental records were scoured in the hope of finding out who she was. However, it was later revealed that her head had not been found. The corpse had been decapitated. But DNA was recovered from the bones.

'Whilst we will make every effort to identify the second person as soon as possible, if you are concerned about someone who is missing, the charity Missing People offers a specialist support service for families and relatives of missing people and for the 250,000 people who go missing each year in the UK,' Fulcher said. 'The inquiry team are liaising with the National Policing Improvement Agency's Serious Crime Analysis Section and the national DNA database in connection with the bones recovered from Eastleach. The police search at the site is expected to continue for the time being. We are making every effort to identify the second person as soon as possible.'

He repeated his appeal for anyone out 'lamping' or poaching, and all gamekeepers in the area had been questioned as the suspect believed that he had been spotted when moving Sian's body.

'Halliwell must have panicked and he decided to move the body late on Tuesday night or the early hours of Wednesday morning,' said the police. 'He seriously thought a gamekeeper had rumbled him. We went to every gamekeeper in the Ramsbury area but nobody had been out at that time. So we think he must have seen a poacher or a lamper but maybe they didn't see him. We are not going to press any charges against them. We just want them to come forward.'

On the afternoon of 27 March, the press were given access to the crime scene at Baxter's Farm. Holes that had been dug in the ground had been filled in by a mechanical digger. Meanwhile, a small team of forensic officers were still sifting through a mountain of soil for clues.

Detective Sergeant Mike Rees confirmed that the bones had been found in a shallow grave in the heavy clay there after three days of searching. They had had then been taken away for testing. He still could not say when the victim has died or who they were.

'It has been a painstaking process,' he said. 'Everyone has put in long hours. We want to make sure we do not miss any evidence.'

Initially, they had found a limb about fifteen yards from the side of the lane.

'We were always confident we were going to find what we were looking for,' he said. 'This has all been about bringing peace to the victim while at the same time gathering all the available evidence to bring the offender to justice.'

The following day, flowers were laid by the officers involved in the case next to a wooden cross, a white teddy bear and a flowering blue forget-me-not, with the message: 'To an unknown lady, now you can rest in peace. Wiltshire, Thames Valley and Avon and Somerset Police.'

Thames Valley Police were involved in the investigation because Sian's body was found in Oxfordshire. Avon and Somerset Police were involved because the investigation was technically being carried out by 'Brunel', a police collaboration with neighbouring Wiltshire Police set up in January 2011 to pool the major crime and special branch units of both forces.

Later, a police spokeswoman said: 'We can confirm that work to recover a second body at Eastleach has been completed and the scene released. Forensic investigations to establish the identity of this young woman are ongoing using DNA and the speed of this identification process relies on whether or not we have her DNA on a database. If we don't get a DNA match, further investigations will need to be carried out, which may take some time. The public can be assured that we will of course inform the victim's family wherever possible before releasing any details in the media.

'So far, no progress has been made in identifying the second victim.

'We are not going to get any results until Tuesday at the earliest,' the spokeswoman said. 'We are still trying to pinpoint the age and height of the victim. No nationality has been mentioned.'

Wiltshire Police would give no indication as to who they thought the woman was. They had no outstanding case of a woman missing from the period indicated by Halliwell.

Halliwell was taken to Swindon Magistrate's Court again on Monday, 28 March. This time, he was greeted by a furious mob of about a hundred, shouting threats and abuse. Women were in tears and two men with tattooed faces had to be restrained. They ran up to the van carrying Halliwell and banged on the side. One of them was former boxer Dean Mayo, a close friend of Kevin Reape's family. He punched the van. Extra security had been laid on to deal with the baying mob, who yelled 'hang the bastard' and 'scum'. The crowd had earlier applauded the police, as well as a group of local taxi drivers gathered near the building.

Halliwell entered courtroom two at 10.20 a.m. His handcuffs were removed as he climbed the stairs from the underground cells and stood impassively in the dock flanked by two prison officers. Wearing a dark suit and a blue-and-white-striped shirt and tie, he looked gaunt and hollow-eyed as he stood in the glass–panelled dock beneath a packed public gallery, where onlookers strained to see him. Shortly before the hearing, the courtroom had been switched for one that had a dock with a roof on it in case things were thrown.

One man shouted: 'Can't we just go to the cells and give it to him?' A woman added: 'He has taken an angel from Swindon. She didn't deserve it. There is a lot of hard feeling out there.'

Chairman of the magistrates, Angus MacPherson, warned everyone: 'Please sit quietly and listen to the proceedings. We know it is an emotional time but we need to do this according to best practice and that's to hear everything everyone has got to say. If you do make a noise you will be asked to leave the court.'

The forty people in the public gallery then sat in silence as the proceedings began.

'Are you Christopher John Halliwell?' the clerk of the court asked.

In a low, flat voice, Halliwell replied: 'Yes.'

Clasping his hands in front of him and staring straight ahead, he spoke only to confirm his name, address, date of birth and the name of his barrister. Then the clerk read out the single charge – that he had murdered Sian O'Callaghan between 18 and 25 March that year. Halliwell showed no emotion and was not asked to enter a plea.

Simon Brenchley, prosecuting, said the case would need to be remitted to Bristol Crown Court for bail and preliminary hearings. For the defence, Tony Hine said his client had not requested a bail hearing, but it was a requirement for a crown court judge to issue any bail guidance.

Ordering the defendant to stand, Mr MacPherson said: 'Mr Halliwell, you are being sent for trial at crown court sitting at Bristol. You will be remanded in custody and there can be a bail hearing in that court on March 30, and a preliminary hearing will be held on April 8.'

At this point, members of the public again vented their fury as Halliwell was taken down from the dock after a hearing of just four minutes. Someone yelled: 'Sicko.'

One man shouted: 'If we ever get hold of you we are going to kill you.' Another said: 'Judge, give him bail. We will look after him.' And a snarling woman screamed: 'You are sick.'

Halliwell was led to the police van with a blanket over his head. Once again, the mood turned ugly. One women shouted: 'How would you like it if it was your daughter, you f★★★ing c★★★?' A man screamed: 'Prison is no safety, you've got £150,000 on your head. You are going to die horribly.'

Another yelled: 'Hang the bastard, that's what you want to do to him.' Another: 'An eye for an eye.'

A cordon of twenty-five police officers struggled to hold back the crowd, who attacked the van as he was driven away. A group of men chased it down the road, hurling insults, thumping the windows and kicking the doors – only halting as it picked up speed on a main road. They were seen off by an escort of two police cars and four motorcycle outriders.

There were bursts of applause for police on guard as people shouted 'Thank you boys' at the Wiltshire constables. Others chanted 'Justice for Sian.'

Dean Mayo had used Facebook to urge people to come to the court. He told *The Sun*: 'Feelings are running very high and I wanted to make sure a lot of people were here. We gave the police a round of applause because they have been amazing.'

A source told the newspaper that Halliwell had stopped talking to the police, while speculation about who the second victim was continued. A police spokeswoman said: 'At the moment we have no idea who she is or what her nationality is.'

The police renewed their appeal for sightings of the green Toyota Avensis estate the night Sian went missing and were continuing to hunt for Sian's clothes, boots, watch, mobile phone and handbag. These were thought to have been dumped along the side of the road to the east of Swindon.

After the hearing, Sian's father Mick spoke publicly at a press conference for the first time to pay tribute to his daughter. He wore a dark suit and an open-neck white shirt; his face was etched with pain. With his son Liam by his side, he fought back the tears, saying: 'You may have to be a bit patient, I'm afraid.'

Composing himself, he read a statement: 'As a family we wanted to express a few words about our beautiful daughter, a wonderful sister to Liam, Lora and Aiden, and loving girlfriend to Kevin. Sian was a bubbly, friendly, caring and loving girl. She was instantly likeable, beautiful and considerate. Although our pain at this time is raw and overwhelming, our memories of Sian will be a comfort to us in the dark days ahead.'

Fighting to keep his voice steady, he continued: 'We would like to firstly thank Steven Fulcher and his team for their exhaustive work in finding and bringing Sian back to us so speedily. Elaine and I, Kevin, Liam, Lora and Aiden would like to thank all our friends and family for their continued support. Words cannot express how comforting this has been for us. We would also like to thank the community in Swindon for their overwhelming kindness and support. The sheer numbers of people involved in the searches, the vigils, flowers, lantern lighting and murals to Sian are incredibly touching and beautiful. Thank you. It only leaves me to say a thank you to the press and media for their respect of our privacy for us as a family at this dreadful time and may we ask you to continue that respect of privacy for the coming, difficult months.'

The family also released a photograph of Sian with Liam, Lora and their youngest brother, ten-year-old Aiden, at a wedding. It showed a scene of family happiness, with all four of them smiling for the camera.

Liam put a comforting arm around his dad's shoulders before the two men left the room. Later, Liam paid his own tribute to Sian, saying: 'She had a spring in her step which she took everywhere and was an inspiration to all who knew her. I am honoured to have been her brother and will cherish the memories I have and shared with my sis.'

Dean Mayo was organising a march around Swindon in Sian's memory that night, starting a Suju at 8 p.m. It would last two hours.

'I only knew Sian a tiny bit but I know her boyfriend Kev and his brother,' he said. 'We want local taxi drivers to know we have respect for them and the police have been amazing. I'm so proud to be part of Swindon.'

Hundreds of mourners would turn out to walk around Old Swindon, retracing some of Sian's final steps, holding photographs and candles. Mayo wrote on Facebook: 'This is where once again Swindon can come together and become one and show our respects to a Swindon Angel.'

A Facebook group called Swindon's Angel was set up, where people could post ideas for remembering Sian. Sian's younger brother Aiden joined in the Facebook tributes. Just hours after she was found dead, he wrote: 'I love you Sian', along with three kisses, on his Facebook page. At 10.23 p.m. on 24 March, he changed his status picture to one of him with the sister he adored at a wedding.

Aiden's moving tribute sparked a spate of touching responses. Friend Rich Deacon wrote: 'She'd be proud so proud of you Aiden. Thinking of you big man.' Lisa Nottage added: 'Hi there little man, I have not stopped thinking about you, ur mum and ur family all week. My heart aches for ur sad loss. Much love to u, ur mum and family.' While Charlotte Landers said: 'Love you Aiden, even though I do wind you up.'

CHAPTER SEVEN

TEARS AND TRIBUTES

On 30 March 2011, Halliwell swept up to Bristol Crown Court from Horfield jail, now known as HMP Bristol, in a cavalcade of police vehicles shortly before 10.30 a.m. But there was no repeat of the angry protests that had taken place in Swindon, though some ten press photographers fought for a shot of him inside the prison van. They were unsuccessful, as the police had decided to bring Halliwell to the court in a special anti-terrorist vehicle with a separate inner cell inside the blacked-out windows.

Several police motorcycles led the motorcade. Bringing up the rear was a black BMW X5 sports utility vehicle containing armed-response police officers. A police riot van full of officers was also stationed outside the court following scenes at Swindon Magistrates' Court two days earlier and the remark made there that there was a £150,000 price on Halliwell's head.

'The Irish community have all got together to put this up,' said Dean Mayo, making it clear that he had not put the money up himself. 'I know people have already been contacted. There are big bets going up within the Irish community on how long Halliwell will last in prison.'

Speaking of the demonstration he had organised outside Swindon Magistrates' Court, he said: 'It was really hard because we didn't want to hurt the police officers. They have been beautiful and we have so much respect for them. The original plan was to turn the police van over, but that didn't happen.'

At the hearing in Court One, Halliwell wore a dark grey suit, white shirt and sky-blue tie, and appeared to have lost weight. He was flanked by four security guards and spoke only to confirm his identity. Rachel Robertson, prosecuting, requested that Halliwell be remanded in custody, while Halliwell's barrister, Daren Samat, said no application for bail would be made.

'I'm quite satisfied that bail is inappropriate given the nature and circumstances of the alleged offences,' said Mr Justice Burnett, and he ordered Halliwell to be remanded in custody until his next appearance via video on 8 April.

During the six-minute hearing, Halliwell again showed no emotion, but instead of staring straight ahead this time he glanced towards the packed press bench and turned his head to look briefly at the ten people in the public gallery.

Afterwards, Halliwell was held in a local police station, rather than being taken back to Horfield, for his own safety.

'The police are taking no chances with all that's surrounding him,' an insider said.

While investigations to establish the identity of the second victim continued, sisters Maria and Julia Grassi paid their respects at the spot in the field now marked by a cross and flowers, where the deceased's remains had been found. They had played there together as children.

Fifty-seven-year-old mother-of-two Maria said: 'We grew up in the village and our father Erminio worked on a local farm for thirty years. We were very shocked to hear about the body being found here – it's beautiful scenery and a very secluded spot. It is all so sad. This woman is somebody's daughter and maybe she is someone's mother as well. It is terrible to think there is a family who won't even know she is dead.'

Meanwhile, Sian's heartbroken mother Elaine was given a last photograph of her daughter. It was taken by one of the friends she was out clubbing with the night she died. 'I've given it to Sian's mum,' said Kate McLeod. 'I wanted the picture to be something she could remember her by.'

Elaine then released other pictures of Sian – one, aged eleven, in her Brownie uniform. Another showed her as a smiling eight-year-old getting ready for a fancy-dress party. She was wearing bright lipstick, two strings of pearls and her mother's sleeveless black dress, which trailed down to her white ankle socks. Then there was one showing her aged nineteen after her sister Lora's prom in July 2008.

At last, Elaine felt strong enough to talk about her daughter to the press. She spoke of the anguish the family had felt when Sian had gone missing and described how she had clung to the possibility that Sian would be found alive.

'I always had hope but I still tried to prepare myself for the worst,' she said. 'When the detective, Steve Fulcher, told us, there were mixed feelings. It was the worst of the worst that

I could've imagined, but they'd found her. That's what I felt when he said it, "They've got her back." Her dad – Mick – shook his hand and thanked him for finding our daughter. It was a relief in a way. I would have hated to live the rest of my life looking over my shoulder and looking at every brunette girl, wondering if that was her. I don't know how other parents can cope with not knowing. I can't imagine never having closure.'

Elaine said that when her daughter was reported missing she believed she was staying with friends, but as the hours passed, it dawned on her that she could be in danger.

'It was what everybody says it is – a rollercoaster,' she said. 'It was mixed feelings and I was trying not to give up hope but also trying to prepare for the worst at the same time. One minute you are thinking she will be OK and then you feel something else the next. I really started to worry when it got to seven or eight o'clock on Saturday evening. During the day, we stayed hopeful. I kept saying, "I bet she has gone with her mates." I did not get the phone call and start panicking straight away.'

Elaine was out of town with her partner, Pete Shaw, the night Sian went missing.

'Me and Pete were away on that Friday and I got the call from her brother Liam at about nine o'clock on Saturday morning,' she said. 'But when I woke up on Sunday morning, I knew this was not Sian. I still had hope, but I had to try and get myself prepared for the worst. To be honest, I just kept going over the facts, and logic made me prepare. I thought, "Would Sian have not been in touch with anyone of her own free will?" And by Sunday I realised Sian would not do it of her own free will – she would not leave Kevin to worry like that. You know your kids – wherever she was it was not her choice.'

By Monday, Elaine's mind was racing and she began to believe that her daughter had been kidnapped.

'I was thinking if we do get her back, we are going to hear some horrible things,' she said. 'When you know that her picture is all over the papers and the television your logic just says, "She is not ignoring this – how could she be?" I knew that if she could have done she would have got in touch.'

Then came the terrible moment when Detective Superintendent Fulcher arrived at the family's home to tell them that Sian was dead.

'Steve Fulcher came out personally at around 3.20 p.m. last Thursday,' she said. 'I remember it exactly because Aiden was supposed to be coming home from school so we had to divert him away. He obviously cared. He kept using the words, "We want to get Sian back to you." And that's how I felt when he told us, "They've got her back."'

Elaine also said that her daughter was happy with her boyfriend, Kevin Reape.

'They had a lovely relationship,' she said. 'They were very together but had their own space. I actually could not understand what took them so long to move in together. It was about three years before they decided to move in together in January. They said they were going to talk about it in the summer and then while they were on holiday last September.'

Then they made the big step. Sian was looking forward to one day starting her a family of her own.

'She loved kids and would've loved to have had kids of her own,' said Elaine. 'She would have been an excellent mum. She was very much a go-with-the-flow type of person and had a very happy nature. She lived for the day. I can't think of any times when she was short-tempered.'

She remembered the fondness Sian had shown her siblings.

'I can remember when Aiden stayed over with her a few weeks ago,' she said. 'Sian brought him home on the Sunday and said she enjoyed it because it gave her an excuse to eat junk food. I will always remember her being happy and upbeat.'

Elaine was also touched by the tributes of well-wishers.

'Sian would be truly moved beyond words at the outpouring of love from everyone,' she said. 'It said a lot about Sian and how highly she was thought of. It makes me feel really proud of her.'

Asked whether she had visited the beauty spot where her daughter's body had been found, she said: 'I haven't been to Uffington. I feel that is something I will want to do in my own time. I don't want to go there at the moment. I don't know when I will – but I might just wake up one day and want to go.'

However, she had made the pilgrimage to Suju with her son Aiden to see the tributes there.

'I wanted to see the candles – that was the nicest bit for me,' she said. 'Sian's little brother Aiden has got his own candle and they have made it so that it stands out from the rest. When we went into the shop to buy the card and flowers we saw the front pages of all the papers on the bottom shelf and started to cry. The woman in the shop realised who we were and told us not to worry about paying for them. In a funny way I would say that was probably the hardest moment so far – writing on the card. What do you say?'

Her highest praise was for the police.

'They have been brilliant, right from the start,' she said. 'They have been sensitive and very honest.'

Elaine's distress was compounded by news that the ashes of convicted paedophile Robert Excell, who had spend thirty-seven years in jail in Australia for abusing boys before being deported to the UK, had been scattered by his widow at Uffington, close to where Sian's body was found. This sparked fury among child-protection groups.

'It is disgusting that other people must pay the price for this man's selfish misdeeds,' said Shy Keenan, a campaigner for the charity Phoenix Chief Advocates. 'Mrs Excell should not have used a family-orientated beauty spot to spread his vile ashes. Our only comfort is the rain will wash him away soon enough.'

Members of O'Callaghan family did not attend the inquest into Sian's death, which was formally opened and adjourned at Oxford Coroner's Court on 1 April. In the ten-minute hearing, Coroner Nicholas Gardiner said examinations were still going on to determine exactly how the young woman died.

'I think the actual cause of death has not yet been defined but is likely to be head injuries of some description,' he said. Home Office pathologists were continuing their investigations.

Sian's body had been formally identified by Pete Shawe, her mother's partner, who had known Sian for four years. Elaine had been too upset to face the ordeal. The hearing was held in order to expedite the funeral arrangements, though Sian could not be buried until Halliwell's defence team had decided whether to request a second post-mortem examination, as was their right.

Outside court, Detective Superintendent Fulcher said Sian's family were bearing up.

'It is a horrific trauma for them,' he said. 'I want them to have closure and they need to organise her funeral. That can't happen until the defence have decided whether or not they want to have a second examination.'

Halliwell's solicitors had twenty-eight days after they had been presented with the results of the first post-mortem to submit a request for another autopsy. In the end, they waived this right.

The following day, after the two-minute silence at Swindon Town's County Ground, a statement from Sian's family was read out, saying: 'We'd like to express our sincere thanks to Swindon. Sian would be moved beyond words at the response.'

Sian's funeral was to be held that Thursday. Sian's mother explained in the *Swindon Advertiser* that provision had been made for local people to pay their respects.

'The cortege will pass slowly through the town, which we felt was an expression of thanks to people who have shown their support,' Elaine said. 'We want the service to be dignified and the family and Sian's boyfriend Kevin ask that our privacy is respected. The cortege will not stop at any point on the route but it will slow down for people who wish to pay their respects.'

Elaine also thanked people who had joined in the search for her daughter, but said she wanted to keep the service private. She requested any donations be made to charities, including Victim Support, Missing Persons, Wiltshire Search and Rescue, and the Prospect Hospice. The £3,000 already raised by events, including the lantern service held in Sian's memory, would be used to create a permanent memorial to her.

More than five hundred people lined the streets of Old Swindon and threw flowers as the cortege passed by with its police escort. Alongside the coffin in the hearse was the name 'Sian' spelled out in white chrysanthemums. Workers left their offices and shops to stand in silent tribute. Others emerged from cafes and pubs. Many were in tears. As the cortege passed the Suju nightclub, mourners tossed dozens of red, yellow and white roses. Some hugged each other for comfort and one tearful woman shouted: 'God bless you, Sian.'

Among the mourners lining the route was twenty-two-year-old Kylie Montgomery.

'We went to school together and we were in a couple of classes together,' she said, fighting back the tears. 'We drifted apart after school but she was a fantastic and amazing woman. And now she's just been taken. It's so sad in just such horrible circumstances.'

Another women said, wiping away tears with a tissue: 'I used to work with her but I don't really want to talk about it.'

Fellow school friend Melloney Welch, twenty-three, said: 'Sian was just a friend of everyone's. If anyone knew her they only had good things to say about her. Today was just lovely that so many people came out to pay their respects.'

Susie Rathbone said: 'A lot of us have already been touched by what's happened to Sian and to her family. I think that we all felt it could have affected any one of us. I came here to show my support to the family and that Swindon does care about these people.'

Sian's friend forty-three-year-old Anna Church, who was giving out flowers, added: 'It just breaks my heart.'

Another friend, twenty-three-year-old Vicky Lawrence, wept and said: 'I just wanted to come here today to say goodbye. I think this was a really nice thing for her parents to do. It allows them to grieve in private at her funeral and allows everyone else to also say goodbye. Sian was a lovely person – really caring.'

Sian's flower-strewn coffin was then taken to Kingsdown Crematorium, where a private service was held for ninety close friends and family. The family looked sombre when they arrived. Aiden was in tears as he and his mum looked at the floral tributes to his big sister. A bunch of pink and white chrysanthemums lay next to the coffin. It was from Elaine and the message read: 'My lovely daughter, miss you always, Mum.'

On Kevin's floral tribute, the note said: 'To my gorgeous Sian, I miss you more than I ever could of imagined.'

CHAPTER EIGHT

THE LIFE AND DEATH OF A SEX WORKER

On 1 April, when the inquest on Sian was opened, *The Sun* was again reporting that the second victim was a prostitute. An unidentified source said that Halliwell met her in the red-light areas of Swindon.

'He said he was trawling the streets until he found one he fancied,' the source said.

Three days later came news that the second victim had been identified from DNA records and Wiltshire Police were trying to trace her family before telling the public.

'We are able to confirm that positive identification has now taken place in relation to the remains discovered in Eastleach,' said a spokesman. 'Work is ongoing to inform the next of kin and immediate family members and as such I'm sure you will appreciate that we are unable to confirm identification at this stage. Further information will be released when possible.'

He added that the chance of a mismatch was one in a billion.

Breaking the bad news again fell to Detective Superintendent Fulcher.

'I have informed some of her family – particularly her mother – but it's too early to identify her publicly,' he said. However, it was confirmed that she came from Swindon.

The following day, the police announced the name of the second victim. It was Becky Godden-Edwards, who had gone missing eight years earlier after falling prey to drug addiction and becoming estranged from her family.

A short statement from her family said: 'The family is completely devastated by the news of Becky's death and at this time wish to be left alone to grieve for our beautiful daughter.'

Her naked body was found in a shallow grave, covered with a thin layer of topsoil less than a foot thick. No trace of her clothes had been found.

'We were able to provide a positive hit from the DNA database and identify that body as that of Rebecca Godden-Edwards, known to her family and friends as Becky,' said Fulcher. 'It was Becky's birthday yesterday and she would have been twenty-nine years old. As you will appreciate, Becky's family and loved ones are trying to come to terms with this devastating news and we are affording them all the comfort and sympathy we can at this time, helping them come to terms with their grief. I'm sure you will join with me in extending our deepest sympathies to the Edwards family.'

The police said Becky Godden had grown up in the Shaw area of Swindon with her father John Godden, mother

Karen and older brother Steven. However, John left home when Becky was six and Steven nine. After divorce, Becky's mother remarried, becoming Karen Edwards, when Becky was fifteen. Becky then lived with her mother, a hairdresser, and her stepfather Charles Edwards, who owns an amusement arcade, in a four-bedroomed converted farmhouse on the edge of town. It was full of photographs of Becky as the pretty, sweet-natured girl she had been before drugs alienated her from her family. She was petite and vulnerable. Full grown she was just four feet eleven inches, with size three feet, and wore children's clothes.

When heroin addiction took hold, she left home and found refuge with pal Hayley Jayne Lowry. In May 1997, she moved in with her dad, who still lived in Swindon, eventually moving on from there too, before disappearing completely.

'She came from a lovely family who were devastated by the loss,' the police said. 'There was such a strong reaction when the message was delivered. They still lived in hope that she would perhaps be reconciled one day. It will take them a long time to come to terms with her death.'

The picture of Miss Godden's life before her disappearance was unclear.

'She got into drug abuse and got into a downward spiral. She was living a chaotic lifestyle. Her family knew that she had drifted into drug abuse. Her grandparents said she was a lovely young girl until various parties got their claws into her.'

The police said they were unable to comment on whether she had been working as a prostitute before her death. They added: 'It's certainly an area we're looking into, but her family aren't aware of anything like that. She was petite, blonde, pretty and from a lovely family. She was a beautiful girl. It's a crying shame it came to this.'

The family lost contact with Becky in 2002 after she got hooked on drugs. She was last seen on 1 January 2003, getting into a taxi outside a nightclub in Swindon, after a night out with friends. Two days later, Halliwell visited his GP with a swollen hand and scratches to his face. He was described as 'emotionally distressed and upset' and told his doctor he had been in a fight with a customer who had started kicking his taxi.

Initially, Becky's family did not report her as missing, as they thought she had moved to London or Bristol. It was not until four years later that they reported her missing to the National Missing Persons Helpline. The following year, her disappearance was reported to the police, but she was not put on the missing person's list due to a red herring, as her grandfather mistakenly believed he had seen Becky in the street two years earlier.

'My biggest fear was that she'd died from a drugs overdose, but we kept hearing until quite recently that Becky had been seen in Bristol,' said her mother, Karen. 'One acquaintance even told us he'd given her a lift and she was pregnant.'

The family had discussed hiring a private detective and kept up the search themselves. In 2010, Becky's mother posted a message on the website missing-you.net. It read: 'Karen Edwards is trying to trace the location of Becky she has been missing for 8 years, and I need to contact her urgent or just to know that she is ok! can anyone help? she could also be in the Bristol area.'

By the time her body was found, the trail had grown cold and detectives appealed for witness to help them piece together her movements.

'At this stage it isn't clear how Becky came to meet her death but further work is ongoing to help us determine this,' Fulcher told reporters. 'Inquiries are continuing to establish the circumstances surrounding Becky's disappearance and subsequent death. Part of these inquiries will be to speak to Chris Halliwell and then we will make a decision on any appropriate steps to take. What I am appealing for is for anyone who knew Becky Godden-Edwards from 2002 onwards, who may have information to help the investigation, if they would please contact the police or indeed *Crimestoppers*. What I am interested in is Becky's movements, her friends, her lifestyle, any small piece of information which may help me piece back together how she came to meet her death. I will respect confidences where people ask for it.'

When the police spoke to Halliwell, he was less than helpful. Asked if he had met Becky Godden when she was working on the streets of Swindon, he replied: 'No comment,' as he was legally entitled to.

The officers asked him if he knew Miss Godden. He replied: 'No… never met her as far as I know.'

They asked him if he had killed the twenty-year-old and again he simply said: 'No comment.'

While Becky's immediate family kept a dignified silence, her grandfather spoke up, saying he wanted to shoot whoever murdered her. Sixty-nine-year-old retired roof tiler Morris Brown added that her family had never given up hope of missing Becky being found alive.

'Only a couple of days ago I was telling my brother what I'd like to do to Sian's killer. I told him, "Give me a shotgun, I'd pull the trigger,"' said Brown. 'And now I find out that Becky has been killed as well – and I feel exactly the same.

Capital punishment is too good for whoever took away that beautiful, bubbly girl from the world. But they'll end up just saying he's sick in the head and put him in a mental hospital. I can't believe she's dead. It's terrible for the family. Her mother, Karen, has been searching for her for such a long time, always hoping that one day she'd come back to the family home. She never once thought anything terrible had happened to her, let alone be found dead like this.'

He added: 'I am devastated. When I knew her she was a bubbly girl. Karen didn't give up hope she'd come home.'

Brown also knew the parents of Sian's boyfriend, Kevin. He had once worked as a subcontractor for the building firm they ran: 'They were a good, hard-working Irish family. My condolences go out to them.'

In the seemingly close-knit town of Swindon, had Becky known Chris Halliwell, he was asked.

'I wouldn't like to say. She knew lots of people,' he replied.

Becky's tearful aunt Lynn Ellis also spoke out.

'She was a lovely girl,' she said. 'The whole family is in pieces.'

Becky's uncle David Godden said from his home in Normanton, Derbyshire: 'It's a bolt from the blue. We'd no idea she was dead. She was a nice girl and she might have fallen in with a bad crowd and gone off the rails. She was a beautiful, blonde girl. My brother always hoped that there would be a reconciliation one day.'

With about twenty friends and relatives, Karen visited the field where Becky's body had been found, and left a card saying: 'When you were born and put into my arms, I cried with joy. I love you so much. But today I am crying for you, my beautiful girl. I loved you the day you were born and I love you even more today. I was always there for you, my baby girl, words can't be said about how I feel. Sleep tight my darling. Love Mum and Charlie.'

Other cards read: 'You will always be in our hearts. Never Forgotten' and 'Rest in Peace'. As the family paid their respects, they stood together with their arms around one another and hugged. They stayed at the field for fifteen minutes before driving away. Other than that, the Edwards family were determined to keep a low profile. They issued a statement saying: 'We are completely devastated by the news of Becky's death and at this time wish to be left alone to grieve for our beautiful daughter.'

And a note was pinned to the gate of the family home saying: 'Please respect our privacy and let us grieve in peace.'

Becky's friend, twenty-eight-year-old Hayley Jane Lowry, wrote on the Facebook page RIP Rebecca Godden: 'I love u Becky. I remember u wanted to be sisters and wish u stayed at mine... why did u lose contact. I wud never have let this happen.'

The family also released two photographs of Becky – one at her mother Karen's wedding, when she was fifteen, and another three years later. Time had taken its toll. The second photograph showed a woman with a drawn face and dyed hair, looking much older than eighteen.

The reason her DNA was on record was because she was convicted of burglary and theft in 2002. She admitted breaking into the Trout Inn in Lechlade, Gloucestershire, twelve miles from Swindon, on 30 May 2001 and stealing a hundred packets of cigarettes, £25 in cash and a handbag containing £18. Her lawyer told Swindon magistrates that she had been taking Class A drugs since she was fifteen. She had been introduced to them by a boyfriend. Another boyfriend had forced her to break into the pub with him after holding a knife to her throat. She was then just nineteen.

Wiltshire Police praised the work of LGC Forensics, whose analysis of the DNA recovered from Baxter's Farm led to Becky being identified. The technique they used involved cleaning up tiny amounts of DNA, copying it and concentrating it.

Due to the length of time her body had been in the ground, others tests were unable to establish a cause of death. But police believed she had been murdered in 2003 and that she had been sexually assaulted before her death. They would speak about the matter to Halliwell, who was then being held in Long Lartin maximum-security prison near Evesham in Worchestershire. They also asked people to think back, just in case – perhaps without realising it – they had seen Becky being abducted or attacked, and they were continuing to liaise with other forces over other unsolved killings. Police were reviewing the death of Melanie Hall and seven other murders in the Swindon area over the previous years, and they would investigate the possibility that there were further unnamed victims.

'We are looking at who else could have been a victim like Becky without being reported missing because of estrangement from their family and so on,' the police said. 'A timeline is being sorted out to establish where Halliwell was, and when, in relation to other cases. They may go back over the last twenty years.' In the event no evidence was discovered linking Halliwell with any other crime.

An insider told *The Sun*: 'There could be other victims. They are preparing to go back over the last twenty years.

When he was first picked up he did chat to detectives, although he has subsequently stayed silent.'

Professor Adrian West, one of the UK's leading criminal psychologists, who created criminal profiles for some of the most infamous murder cases in British history, including Jill Dando, would also help police in their preparations to interview Halliwell, though a spokeswoman for Wiltshire Police said he would not be interviewing any suspects.

Five days later, fifty-one-year-old Karen Edwards found the strength to talk about the death of her daughter after her descent into drug addiction. Flanked by her husband Charlie and sister Tracy Mullane, she cried as she described Becky as a loving child who became a different person when she began taking drugs as a teenager.

'Becky gave me so much joy and love as a child,' she said. 'However, as a teenager, she got involved with people who introduced her to drugs. She left school and her life spiralled into some very dark places to feed her addiction. She became a different person.'

The family had battled for years to combat her drug problem.

'During her teenage years we did everything we could to help her overcome her drug addiction,' she said. 'We sought help from drug charities, doctors. We also asked for help from MP Julia Drown. We then put her into a private rehabilitation centre.'

Nothing did any good, but still the family strived to protect Becky from herself.

'We tried everything to stop Becky from leaving home,' Karen said. 'But on every occasion the pull of her habit was stronger and she would do whatever she had to, to get her next fix. It was not unusual behaviour for Becky to disappear for weeks or months on end.'

Somehow, they managed to stay in touch.

'When Becky was in serious trouble she always phoned me and usually my husband, my sister or her brother or me would go and get her and bring her home, only for her to disappear again,' said Karen. 'Life was very tough for all of us and we witnessed many awful things that we would not wish on any parent.'

Karen said her daughter wanted to turn her life around following her conviction for theft in 2001 and decided to leave home rather than cause more trouble for her family.

'Becky told me once that she loved me so much she could not keep putting me through hell and she was leaving and would not come home until she was clean,' she said. 'I never saw her again but I thought she was living in Bristol, where she had been before. Over the years, I have tried to find her through the police, the hospital and other organisations that trace missing persons, but to no avail. I was told by sources close to the family, time and time again, that they had seen Becky during the missing years, so I had a strong belief, and really did believe, that one day she would come back home. Becky was loved by all her family and our loss is unbearable.'

Karen continued buying her birthday cards, Christmas presents and cards – 'so that when she did come back home she knew I had been thinking of her every year since she left, hoping for one day that I would be able to give them to her,' she said.

The police brought news of her death on what would have been Becky's twenty-ninth birthday. When the officers arrived on her doorstep, Karen said she knew instantly why they had come.

Eleven days earlier, she had seen on TV that murder squad detectives digging up a field in Eastleach had found a girl's dismembered body.

'I had a gut feeling it was Becky,' she said. 'Call it mother's instinct. She had been missing too long. I will never forget that day. I had spent the morning helping Steven decorate his new home. We were laughing and joking because I was wearing pink wellies and a tracksuit. We went back home at lunchtime to put the kettle on and from then on my life as I knew it changed.'

Until then, she still nurtured hope – a hope that was snuffed out by the arrival of the police.

'Life was hard before, when we thought she was living the life of an addict,' she said. 'But we really did think she was alive and that one day she would come back home. Becky has now been found and the news of her horrific death has devastated all her family.'

Paying tribute to her daughter, Karen said: 'Becky was a very beautiful, intelligent girl. She was loved by all her family and we all loved her with all our hearts.'

She went on to thank Wiltshire Police. She also sent her condolences to Sian O'Callaghan's family. 'We know what they are going through,' she said.

As she spoke, friends of Becky released two hundred helium balloons carrying her picture in Queen's Park, Swindon, in her memory.

Later, John Godden made a tribute to his daughter.

'At this moment in time I am unable to face the press and the world,' he said. 'I would like to say a few words about

Becky my daughter, who I regarded as Miss World. I am a shattered man and nothing seems worthwhile. Becky has always been a daddy's girl; she always stood by me through thick and thin. Becky would not have anything said about her dad, I adored her so much she could do no wrong; she will always be Daddy's girl. My sweet angel will never ever be forgotten!!! We had so many lovely times together; Becky was my soul mate and will remain in my broken heart for ever. Lots of love from Daddy xxx.'

The discovery of Becky's remains by police investigating the murder of Sian prompted the newspapers to ask how it was that 250,000 people a year in Britain simply vanished.

Nicki Durbin's son, Luke, a bright, sociable nineteen-year-old, disappeared in May 2006 after going clubbing with friends in Ipswich.

'I know families always say that not one day goes by without them thinking about their loved one. But there's not an hour goes by without me thinking about Luke,' she told *The Guardian*. 'Certain times are very difficult. Anniversaries, or when the season changes. It's another spring or winter that he's not here. I hope I'll see him again, but I know it's not a very realistic hope. I can be working and hear a song in the background and I'm thinking of Luke and I have to keep functioning.'

Nicki, a charity fundraiser, said she found herself glued to the television when a big missing person story was in the news. When a body was found – as in Becky's case – she felt relief if it turned out to be a woman's. Then she felt something akin to envy, as at least the family had found out what happened to their loved one. Over the years, her confidence in the police has eroded. At times, she felt they were not listening to her and Luke's friends. She had to scream to get her son's case taken on by Suffolk's major investigation team.

She accepted it was likely that Luke was dead.

'If that is the case, please let it have been an accident. If someone else is involved it's just too horrifying,' she said. The best scenario for her was that Luke went off and was living a fantastic life somewhere. 'And if he ever comes home he'll get the biggest slap of his life – and then the biggest hug.'

According to the National Police Improvement Agency, which runs the national missing persons bureau, police file about a thousand missing reports every day, although some refer to the same person. Most missing persons return home or are found quickly. Around twenty people a week are found dead, while almost two thousand cases a year remain outstanding. In fact, the total number of missing people is bigger than that, as the NPIA's data is not complete, partly because not all forces handed in their figures.

A study by researchers at York University estimated that two thirds of those who go missing decide to go. A fifth 'drift' away. One per cent are 'forced', while of the rest are unintentionally absent – they have mental health problems, for example.

The charity Missing People has proposed that every region have a missing persons' co-ordinator, and every family have a single point of contact in the police force dealing with their case. It also wants a network of counsellors to help those left behind.

'It is incredible that in England and Wales we have no legislation relating to missing people. It is an issue that has been hidden for a long time,' said the charity's then chief executive Martin Houghton-Brown.

Missing People also wants the families of people who were missing to be given the same rights as victims of crime.

'If your DVD player is stolen from your house, you'll get a letter from the police detailing all the help you can get. If your child goes missing you may get nothing,' Houghton-Brown said.

Peter Lawrence, the father of the chef Claudia Lawrence, who went missing from York in 2009, said he was 'amazed at the problems facing families of missing people. If you're the subject of a minor crime, the state gives you support. If someone goes missing there's nothing.'

Rachel Elias, the sister of Manic Street Preachers' guitarist Richey Edwards, who vanished in 1995, complained that there was a lack of sympathy and understanding when it came to missing adults.

'I think it's because of the sheer number of adults who go missing,' she told *The Guardian*. 'There's also the feeling that many people choose to go missing and should be allowed to.'

Another complaint was the lack of consistency over how missing people's cases are handled.

'There should be a single contact with the police. Different forces seem to do it all in different ways, which is frustrating,' she said.

CHAPTER NINE

INADMISSIBLE EVIDENCE

On 8 April 2011, Halliwell appeared for the five-minute preliminary hearing at Bristol Crown Court via videolink from Long Lartin prison. He spoke three times to confirm he could hear proceedings, to confirm his name and to say he understood what the judge said.

Prosecutor Ian Lawrie, QC, told the court: 'As the court will know, another lady has been found and identified and it is the police's intention to interview Mr Halliwell in respect of that young lady. That will be done in the next few weeks and I simply mention it because, depending on how that interview goes, there will be a Crown application to connect matters.'

Mr Justice Burnett remanded Halliwell in custody until a plea and case management hearing, to be held on 14 July. Halliwell responded: 'OK, thank you.'

Meanwhile, the police continued hunting for new clues.

They began digging up the front gardens of 12 Ashbury Avenue, where Halliwell had lived with Heather Widdowson, and number 24, where he had lived with his first wife Lisa. Officers used a radar device to scan for any large objects beneath the surface of the ground, while a female civilian worker logged their progress using a laptop computer. Of particular interest was the hole, fifteen feet wide and five feet deep, Halliwell had dug in the back garden of number 24, saying it was for a trampoline. He had then asked his former father-in-law Tony Byrne's building firm to fill it in with concrete. It was later covered by a lawn.

Halliwell had once worked for his father-in-law's business, Byrne & King Ltd, and the police were tracing where he travelled to while with the firm. Mr Byrne refused to comment.

Both houses had been thoroughly searched, but the police denied that they were trying to trace all forty of the cars that Halliwell had owned at one time or another. It later transpired that he had owed more than eighty cars during his career as a cabbie and the police did take an interest. Meanwhile, the police were taking a special interest in Halliwell's then current address, number 12.

Halliwell himself was saying nothing, so two months after Sian had gone missing, his ex-wife sent a letter begging him: 'Tell us what happened.'

Lisa was keen to know if he had killed any other women and urged him: 'Put us out of our misery.'

Seventeen-year-old Carissa, the youngest of their three children, then visited him in prison to ask him face-to-face what he had done.

'Lisa and his kids aren't coping well at all – they've put

their lives on hold,' *The Sun* was told by someone close to the family. 'She's written to him begging him to come clean about everything so they can try to put it all behind them and get on with their lives. What they don't want is for one trial to end and for there then to be another in a couple of years' time because that would devastate them all over again... Lisa's letter was short and to the point but they are desperate for answers. They are just in limbo at the moment. Lisa is just begging him to be unselfish. If not for the sake of her, at least for the children.'

Of Carissa's visit shortly after his arrest, the source said: 'She wanted to look him in the eye and hear for herself what he had to say.'

On 24 May, Halliwell appeared in court again, this time in Worcester. He was charged with the murder of Rebecca Godden-Edwards between 27 December 2002 and 1 January 2006. He was wearing a maroon T-shirt and grey trousers. Flanked by two police officers, he spoke only to confirm his name and date of birth. This time, he smirked at the packed press bench and kept the smug expression on his face as he was remanded in custody.

Magistrate Ray Needham adjourned the case for three days until Halliwell appeared at Bristol Crown Court again via video link for a bail hearing. Addressing the defendant, he told him: 'On this charge of murder we are sending you to Bristol Crown Court. You will be remanded in custody until then.'

The hearing took just three minutes.

That Thursday, Halliwell made his video-link appearance at Bristol Crown Court for a ten-minute preliminary hearing. Now looking gaunt and balding, he was seen wearing a grey jumper. He sat behind a table and looked straight ahead towards the video camera. He spoke only three times – to confirm his name, to say he could hear proceedings, and, at the conclusion of the hearing, that he had understood what had been said. The Recorder of Bristol, Judge Neil Ford, QC, said that a plea and case-management hearing had already been fixed for 14 July. He granted a defence application for leading counsel and said the trial would be held the following year.

'What I will say is if this is a contested matter, the case will be tried – unless there is good reason why it shouldn't – in January next year,' he told the court. 'It would have to be tried by a High Court judge.'

No application for bail was made and Halliwell was again remanded in custody.

Meanwhile, the bereft families continued to grieve. On 3 June, Sian's parents held a private ceremony for what would have been her twenty-third birthday. They said: 'We grieve for you in silence and try not to show. But what it meant to lose you, no one will ever know.'

Sian's friend Daniel Hughes wrote on Facebook: 'Hope wherever you are, you're looking down, and feeling the love a lot of people have for you.'

Becky Godden-Edwards' funeral was scheduled for 18 July. Her family said the service would be held at 1 p.m. at Christ Church in Old Town, Swindon, and was open to anyone who would like to attend. More than one hundred and fifty mourners turned out. Police motorcycle outriders escorted the funeral procession.

Friends and family wore pink clothes and flowers, and had tied pink ribbons to their cars at the request of Becky's mum.

It was Becky's favourite colour. The hearse was adorned with floral tributes that spelled out 'Becky' and 'LuLu'. Karen Edwards wept copiously as she watched her daughter's white wicker coffin being carried into the church. Stepfather Charles Edwards was a pallbearer. Her father, John, also attended the service. Before the service, Karen said of Becky: 'She was a free spirit and a little girl who lost her way.'

Lay Minister Margaret Williams, who led the service, said: 'It's always an emotional time, but this one is even more so because of the tragic circumstances of her death. All the time she's been missing, the family never gave up hope. So this, in a way, is their way of welcoming her home.'

A poem was read to the congregation by Becky's cousin Laura, who described her depart relative as 'so glamorous with your long blonde hair and heels'. The congregation sang 'All Things Bright and Beautiful' and 'Amazing Grace'. There was also a personal tribute to Becky on behalf of the family and followed by Elton John's 'Candle in the Wind'. The Westlife hit 'You Raise Me Up' was played as people filed out of the church. A private burial service took place afterwards.

Halliwell's twenty-five-minute administrative hearing did not take place until 28 July 2012. Again he appeared by video link, sitting behind a table in an interview room in Long Latin. He wore a dirty grey jumper with the sleeves rolled up and showed no emotion.

Judge Ford told him again that the case would proceed in front of a High Court judge. 'A High Court judge will take it on and give directions to how the case will continue,' he said. 'I expect this will be towards the end of the year.'

Three days later, Halliwell appeared at Preston Crown Court, where he denied murdering Sian O'Callaghan. Then the charge of murdering Becky Godden was formally removed from the indictment. Mrs Laura Justice Cox DBE ruled that evidence gained following Halliwell's arrest was inadmissible as the police had not followed the provisions of the 1984 Police and Criminal Evidence Act governing the treatment of suspects that protects from 'oppressive' questioning. Halliwell had been denied contact with a solicitor, despite repeatedly asking for one during the four hours after his arrest.

After hearing legal arguments, Mrs Justice Cox said: 'Following Halliwell's arrest on March 24, 2011, there were serious and irretrievable breaches by the senior investigating officer of the mandatory rules governing the detention and interview of arrested suspects by the police.'

She ruled that Detective Superintendent Fulcher had misused clause C.11.1 of the Police and Criminal Evidence Act (PACE), which allows a policeman to put aside PACE if a delay in interviewing the suspect would be likely to lead to harm to evidence or to other people, or serious loss of or damage to property. Mrs Justice Cox decided that this could be used only in relation to the immediate search for Sian O'Callaghan.

'Once the defendant had directed Detective Superintendent Fulcher to the place where Ms O'Callaghan could be located, the relevant risk had been averted and the qualifying criteria for an urgent interview under C.11.1 no longer existed,' she said.

Halliwell should then have been taken to a police station, cautioned and been provided with a lawyer. The prosecution did not oppose an application by Halliwell's defence team to have the charge dismissed. Meanwhile, Fulcher was suspended. Sian's case could continue though, as there was other evidence connecting him to the crime. Forensics had discovered traces of Sian's blood on the seat covers he was seen dumping and CCTV footage had shown him picking her up.

Detective Chief Superintendent Kier Pritchard, head of Wiltshire CID, said that Mr Fulcher's colleagues were upset by his suspension. He said: 'They have to accept the findings of the court. Clearly they are disappointed, that is natural.'

Sian's father, Michael, gave Fulcher a ringing endorsement. He told reporters: 'I want to put on record the wonderful job that Steve Fulcher did finding our daughter so early.'

Becky's family were less sanguine.

'I only found out that Becky's name had been dropped from the indictment twenty minutes before we went into court for the first hearing,' said Karen Edwards. 'The police told me they didn't have enough evidence to charge him with Becky's murder. I remember going to Marlborough police station with my husband Charlie and being asked whether we would be content if he went away for a long time for Sian's murder and the charges against Becky were left on file. My answer to that was, "Never."'

But there was no getting around Mrs Justice Cox's ruling. The charge of murdering Becky Godden would lie on file because Detective Superintendent Fulcher had not followed arrest guidelines. It had been withdrawn as he had breached Halliwell's rights by failing to caution him, and denied him a solicitor in an attempt to force information out of him.

CHAPTER TEN

THE GUILTY PLEA

When Halliwell appeared at Bristol Crown Court on 19 October 2012, he altered his plea to guilty. This change of heart came about, apparently, after his daughter Carissa wrote to him saying: 'You've broken enough hearts, it's time to tell the truth.'

The court heard that Halliwell had signed off from work but, instead of going home, he'd cruised the streets in his green Toyota Avensis taxi looking for a victim. He had switched off the radio so his colleagues at the taxi firm would not know where he was.

After leaving the nightclub, Sian walked past the Goddard Arms on High Street in the Old Town area. Halliwell had stopped and, fatefully, she got into his taxi. He drove Sian to nearby Savernake Forest, where he sexually assaulted her. He had then stabbed and killed her.

Halliwell made four visits to where Sian's body was

hidden in the twenty-four hours after her abduction and murder. In the early hours of 21 March, two days after the slaying, he moved the body from Savernake Forest to Uffington, where he dumped it down a steep bank by the side of a quiet rural road.

The CCTV in the High Street had picked up the number plate on his car and, the following day, he became the prime suspect and was put under surveillance. The court heard that he then put missing posters of the young woman in the back of his taxi even as he tried to clear up traces of her blood inside. He was arrested on 24 March.

After the police first arrested Halliwell, they considered whether there might be other victims as, during their discussion on Sian O'Callaghan's disappearance, he was said to have speculated about there being more bodies. He was alleged to have remarked to a colleague: 'Who knows what or who you find buried out there? There could be loads of people over the years.'

Later that day, he led detectives to Sian's body. She was found face down and naked from her waist to her ankles. There was a bite mark on her left breast. A swab taken from the injury revealed a mixed DNA profile with components from Halliwell. A forensic odontologist inspected the injury but Halliwell refused to supply a dental impression.

A post-mortem examination found that Sian had died from the combined effects of two stab wounds to the head and neck, as well as compression to the neck. The attack had been brutal. There was further evidence of blunt trauma to the back of the head and areas of external deep bruising to her face. The trauma to her head could have been caused either by her falling, by being pushed to the ground, or by her head being forcibly struck by a broad object. This resulted in a fracture to the skull.

The bruising on her body was consistent with being punched or kicked. There was also evidence of bruising to the neck, which could have been caused by either compression, blunt force trauma or a combination of both. Home Office pathologist Dr Amanda Jeffery concluded that those injuries could have been caused by either deliberate strangulation or attempts at restraining the victim by the neck.

'She must have suffered terribly before dying,' said Nick Hawkins, Chief Crown Prosecutor for Wessex. 'Halliwell was the last person in the world you would want to meet on a dark night in Swindon.'

Forensic examination found Sian's blood in the rear of Halliwell's car and police also had CCTV and automatic number-plate recognition evidence to put him in the Old Town area when she vanished.

Halliwell's internet history also revealed he heavily researched rope knots and bondage techniques. Several books on DNA and forensic testing were found in his loft along with a stash of wet wipes.

Detective Chief Superintendent Kier Pritchard said Halliwell had carefully planned Sian's murder and went to lengths to cover his tracks.

'This was a violent and brutal murder of a young woman in the prime of her life,' he said. 'It is likely that Sian suffered horrifically from the point that she was abducted. We can only imagine how Sian suffered in those last moments. Halliwell has shown himself to be a despicable man and has shown no remorse throughout.'

He continued: 'On that night there was clearly an

element of premeditation. He closed his links with the taxi company but continued to cruise the streets of Swindon looking for a victim. He used his position as a taxi driver, with no doubt, to coax Sian into the vehicle. From that moment – abusing that position of trust – he drove her in the opposite direction. He has then used extreme violence in the attack on Sian, culminating in the use of a weapon in the final aspects of her murder. This also had an element of a sexual offence. He then tried to use every opportunity to conceal her murder by moving her body and destroying evidence.

'Christopher Halliwell can only be described as a despicable man and today justice has been delivered and he has been brought to justice for the murder of Sian.'

Pritchard said that the investigation into Rebecca Godden-Edwards' murder would look at whether other people had fallen victim to Halliwell.

'That continues as part of the live investigation,' he said. 'Clearly we would like to bring Becky's killer to justice. Part of the investigation will be to look at whether there are other crimes and other victims. It is very much an open line of inquiry.'

Halliwell's defence counsel, Richard Latham QC, said his client claimed he stabbed Sian O'Callaghan because he became furious when she protested about being taken in the wrong direction after he picked her up in his taxi. As he was still driving, Halliwell said he lost his temper and punched Sian in the face. In the melee of bringing the car to a halt he stabbed her in the head and neck.

Mr Latham, who had successfully prosecuted Soham child killer Ian Huntley, said: 'He took her to Savernake Forest, he dragged her body out of the car, dragged it from the car and abandoned her in the forest at the side of a field.'

Sian's family were in court to see Halliwell plead guilty. They collapsed in tears in the public gallery as their victim-impact statements were read out while Halliwell sat impassively in the dock.

Elaine wrote: 'I'm just a mum who wants her daughter back. There never truly is closure, moving on is accepting that my life has changed in every way.'

Father Mick said: 'My oldest daughter was the most loving, caring daughter any father could wish for.'

And Sian's live-in boyfriend Kevin Reape said: 'My heart was ripped out, my life has been destroyed. Our future together was taken. Sian was a beautiful, happy-go-lucky person who could cheer up the most miserable of people. I shall spend the rest of my life being glad of the time I had with her.'

In sentencing Halliwell, Mrs Justice Cox rejected the account put forward by his counsel. The evidence that the abduction and murder were deliberate was compelling.

'You have pleaded guilty to the murder of Sian O'Callaghan, a much-loved daughter, sister and partner – a happy, lively and caring young woman who enriched the lives of all those who knew her and who had everything to live for,' the judge told Halliwell. 'Your account bears all the hallmarks of an account carefully designed to try and explain away separate aspects of the evidence relied upon by the prosecution. You stopped and no doubt offered her, or persuaded her, to have a taxi ride home, because she got into your taxi. Poignantly, her partner had advised her never to walk home alone but to always use a taxi. She probably had that advice in mind when she got into your taxi, thinking that she would be safe; that it was the right thing to do.

'But she soon would have realised, with horror, that you were not taking her home because you drove off in the opposite direction – out of Swindon towards Marlborough and the Savernake Forest – a distance it would have taken about half an hour to drive.

'Having regard to all the evidence, and in particular the telephone evidence relating to the location of Sian's mobile, I reject the suggestion that you were initially told to drive to Covingham. I am sure you knew exactly what you were doing when Sian got inside your taxi.'

The judge continued: 'What exactly you did to her, and why you did it, may never be known. You went home later that morning, but Sian did not. You had assaulted her and murdered her and you had left her body somewhere in the Forest area. I am entirely satisfied that you intended to kill her.

'On March 24, Sian's body was found, partially concealed amongst the undergrowth and positioned down a steep bank where she would not readily be seen. She was lying face down and she was naked from the waist down to her ankles. Her leggings and underwear were wrapped around her ankles and fabric from these, items of clothing had been cut away in the crotch and buttock areas. Her bra had been removed and a torn bra strap was found in the sleeve of her cardigan.

'The cause of Sian's death was considered to be the combined effects of two stab wounds to her head and neck and compression of the neck. You had stabbed her twice with a knife and there is little doubt that they were the fatal wounds. You admit that you kept a knife in your car for self-protection.'

The judge said that one of the injuries inflicted upon the defenceless victim with the knife would have required 'severe force'. The blade of the six-inch kitchen knife penetrated three-and-a-half inches into her brain.

'These, then, were the physical injuries you inflicted upon that young woman in what was clearly a savage and brutal attack,' Mrs Justice Cox said. 'The pain, terror, anguish and desperation she would have suffered, as you assaulted and then murdered her, is truly horrifying to contemplate.

'But her terror would have started long before then. She would have been terrified and panic-stricken right from the moment she realised that you were not going to drive her home. She was terrified, helpless and alone.'

The judge said that Sian's murder did have a sexual motive.

'After circling the area where you eventually saw Sian, you deliberately abducted this attractive young girl, who was alone late at night, and you drove her some distance away,' Mrs Justice Cox said. 'Her injuries included injuries to her left breast and nipple consistent with bites or another form of aggressive assault. Her body was found half naked, with her leggings and underwear around her ankles. These factors, together with the cutting away of fabric from those items of clothing in the crotch area and the removal of her bra, point clearly to sexual conduct. Had Sian survived, this evidence would have amounted to evidence of a sexual assault.

'There are a number of aggravating features in this case. You abused your position as a taxi driver, in a car clearly marked as a taxi, and as someone Sian thought she could trust. Her abduction was clearly premeditated. As a young woman walking alone late at night and under the influence of drink, she was a vulnerable victim. There was here a prolonged period of time in which she would have suffered extreme fear and terror as well as severe pain from the injuries you inflicted upon her. And you made extensive efforts to conceal her body.

'There is little advanced by way of mitigation. I accept, however, that your plea of guilty has avoided Sian's family having to endure a trial, which is an important factor.'

Halliwell was given a mandatory life sentence for murder. Mrs Justice Cox then had to set a minimum tariff.

'Taking all the relevant factors into account,' she said, 'and having careful regard to the overall seriousness of this offence, the starting point will remain as thirty years. I shall allow a discount of five years for your plea of guilty, taking into account the legal advice you received, entirely properly, and the time that elapsed in this case as a result. There will also be deducted the period of 571 days, which you have already spent in custody. The period will be deducted from the minimum of twenty-five years, which is the term I consider properly reflects the seriousness of this case. If you are eventually released on licence you will remain on licence for the rest of your life.'

Turning to Sian's family, Mrs Justice Cox said: 'I address these remarks to you as throughout the many months that have passed since the death of Sian I acknowledge that you have had to live not only with that tragedy, but with legal argument that you no doubt found complex and delays you found frustrating. You have behaved throughout this case with quiet dignity, patience and courtesy.

'You have had today to listen to details of Sian's last hours, all of which will have been acutely distressing for you. I understand entirely that your lives have been shattered at Sian's loss in such a cruel and pointless way. I pay tribute to you all for everything you have had to endure and the dignified way you have acted throughout this case. Sian can never be restored to you but I hope that you feel that today in this court justice has been served.'

The judge also paid tribute to the very hard work carried out by a team of police officers involved in the investigation into Sian's disappearance and murder.

'Clearly the evidence that accumulated was carefully done, thoughtfully done and extended into a compelling picture,' she said.

Throughout the whole process, Sian's mother Elaine had spared herself no detail.

'I wanted to know everything,' she said. 'I didn't want to be wrapped in cotton wool. I read the entire autopsy report – I needed to know what my daughter had gone through. I also read up about Halliwell and knew there was another victim. For me, I took some comfort in knowing that it was a random attack. I feel like it would have been worse if Sian had known him.'

Elaine told *The Sun* she felt no hatred for her daughter's killer.

'That might be hard for people to understand, but I don't walk around consumed with anger,' she said. 'Sian wouldn't want that. Instead, I feel nothing for him.'

When Halliwell had changed his plead to guilty, Elaine was immediately on the phone to her oldest son.

'As soon as I got the news I phoned Liam, but I couldn't speak, I was crying so much,' she said. 'The emotion that overcame me was surprising, because it came from nowhere.

I was totally together and then as soon as my son answered the phone, I could barely get the words out.'

Outside the court, Detective Chief Superintendent Kier Pritchard read a statement:

'Today, Christopher Halliwell has pleaded guilty to the murder of Sian O'Callaghan on March 19, 2011. Firstly, I'd like to express our deepest sympathy for the family and friends of Sian. I can only imagine how hard the last eighteen months has been for them and how difficult it must have been to have heard in court today how violently Sian was attacked before her death.

'Sian's family and loved ones have shown great dignity throughout the court process, resulting in Halliwell's guilty plea today. I hope this conviction will in some way help the family to move forward with their lives. Sian's disappearance received high-profile media coverage and unprecedented support from the whole community. Hundreds of people went out of their way to help and support Wiltshire Police in our search for Sian, who disappeared after a night out with friends in Swindon.

'Shortly after leaving a local nightclub, Sian was abducted by Christopher Halliwell, a taxi driver. He had booked off-duty but had continued to circle around the area of Old Town, Swindon looking for a victim. After he took Sian, he then drove her to the outskirts of Swindon and into the Savernake Forest area near Marlborough. He violently attacked her, subjected her to a sexual assault and murdered her. Six days later, police officers found her body in a remote location south of Uffington.

'This was a complex and fast-moving investigation and from the outset the priority of the senior investigating officer,

THE GUILTY PLEA

Detective Superintendent Steve Fulcher, was always to try and find Sian alive, but unfortunately this was not possible. This was a violent and brutal murder of a young woman in the prime of her life. It is likely that Sian suffered horrifically from the point that she was abducted.

'Halliwell, in committing this crime, betrayed his position of trust as a taxi driver as he preyed on a lone vulnerable female. Today, the court heard that there was clear evidence of premeditation. We can only imagine how Sian must have suffered throughout this ordeal and in those last moments. Christopher Halliwell went on to conceal Sian's body and attempted to destroy the evidence of his violent crime. He has shown himself to be a despicable man and has shown no remorse throughout. Whilst Halliwell's admission of guilt today may go some way to help the family grieve, it will not bring Sian back, who was needlessly and tragically taken from them.

'Finally, crimes of this nature are extremely rare in Wiltshire and I would particularly like to thank our local communities for their overwhelming support and compassion. Today's hearing was about bringing justice for Sian's family. They have continued to display great courage and dignity and we hope this will provide them with some comfort at this most difficult time.'

Addressing reporters, Sian's mother described her daughter as an incredible person who would continue to inspire her family.

'The devastating loss of Sian in such a brutal way has been for my family, Kevin, and everyone who knew Sian, a burden to live with,' Elaine said. 'The overwhelming response of support has been a comfort to us. Our lives have been changed for ever as a result of a truly wonderful life taken too soon.

She will continue to inspire us and never be forgotten. As her mum, I will remember her as the incredible person that she was. I would like to pay tribute to Sian's brothers and sister for their immense strength, conduct, composure, dignity and support throughout this immensely distressing time.

'There is never total closure, just accepting my life has changed for ever. I am just a mother who wants her daughter back. Christopher Halliwell has by his heinous actions taken my vibrant young daughter and caused unimaginable distress. The sentencing today of Halliwell will not bring Sian back, but will mean he can't take any more. We will all endeavour to get on with our lives, the way Sian would have wanted.'

Sian's father, Mick, welcomed the life sentence for his daughter's killer.

'Justice has been done today,' he said. 'It has been a very emotional day.'

He went on to thank the family's QC, the Criminal Prosecution Service (CPS) and police, especially Detective Superintendent Fulcher, for finding his daughter's body so soon.

'Our thoughts go to Becky's family and hope their conclusion comes as it has for us,' he added.

Becky's mother Karen Edwards tearfully described her family's anguish in an emotional speech about how her daughter had become addicted to drugs but she had never given up hope that one day she would return home to her family. Now she was seeking justice.

'After a very complicated and painful journey over the last eighteen months, Sian's family have today had the justice for murder of their beautiful daughter,' she said. 'But where's the justice for my Becky? Did you see the smirk on Halliwell's face when he was sentenced? That man's so evil he should never walk the streets again. While there is breath in my body, I will strive to get justice for my Becky.

'Our family's fight for justice for Becky has only just begun. Even though Becky has been found, after all this time we still have no full understanding of how she met her death. Wiltshire Police will be continuing the ongoing investigation into my daughter Becky's murder. As you can imagine, this has been a very dreadful time for all our family and I would like to thank everyone for the continued support in our struggle for justice for Becky. I would like the full support of you all to help me get justice for my daughter Becky.'

Detectives wanted to know if Halliwell was a serial killer who used his job as a cabbie to prey on young women. CPS chiefs admitted he would probably have been given a whole-life tariff had they been able to convict him on both murders. As it was, Nick Hawkins, Chief Crown Prosecutor for Wessex, said: 'If he ever comes out of prison, he will be a very old man.'

CHAPTER ELEVEN

JUSTICE FOR BECKY?

In the course of the court proceeding, it was revealed that, during a series of one-to-one interviews over the course of four hours, Halliwell had confessed to murdering Sian O'Callaghan and led Fulcher to her body. He then admitted killing another woman and showed the detective where Becky Godden-Edwards was buried. But the judge said: 'As soon as he began to talk about another offence, it is clear that he should have been cautioned. There should have been no further discussions about it and the defendant should have been taken to the police station.'

During legal wrangling in a preliminary hearing in February, Halliwell's team had insisted that the way in which the evidence was gathered breached the Police and Criminal Evidence Act, which gives any suspect the right to legal advice and to be questioned without oppression. Fulcher's questioning was 'an assault on the integrity of the legal system', said Halliwell's QC, Ian Latham. 'Whether he felt it was morally justified or that it would not do any harm, he should not have done it.'

When asked to justify his tactics, Fulcher said: 'It was my responsibility as the SIO responsible for Sian, for her life or her death. The last thing I could do is speak to him in person and that's what I did.'

He told the court: 'I did think it was utterly ridiculous that someone who took me, twelve people and a surveillance helicopter to the deposition sites of two bodies would then seek to find some loophole or quirk in the law to get away from the fact that he was a multiple murderer.'

His strategy was backed by senior colleagues. Deputy Chief Constable Patrick Geenty said: 'There may be occasions where police officers have to make a decision in terms of saving life to step outside the rules. I think the decision he made was a gutsy decision, a brave one. I would like to think I would make a similar decision in his circumstances, bearing in mind what we had been through trying to find Sian alive.'

However, the trial judge, Mrs Justice Cox, ruled that none of the evidence gathered during the four-hour period when the bodies had been discovered could be used in any trial. That meant the prosecutors were forced to drop the murder charge relating to Becky Godden because they did not have any other evidence that linked him to the killing. Nick Hawkins, the Chief Crown Prosecutor for Wessex, said that as no forensic evidence was found on Becky's remains, the best chance of ever securing a conviction for the killing was if Halliwell confessed to another inmate while serving time in prison.

'We are very much in Mr Halliwell's hands if he wants to volunteer anything,' Mr Hawkins said.

JUSTICE FOR BECKY?

As the judge had ruled that Halliwell's legal rights had been breached by detectives during the course of the investigation, it seemed Becky's family might never know how, when or why she had died. Nor, barring a confession or new evidence emerging, would they ever see her killer held to account.

'What is wrong with this country when Halliwell's rights are more important than ours? He led police to my daughter's body, but he can't be tried for her murder? It doesn't make any sense,' Karen told the *Daily Mail*. 'All we want is justice for Becky. Doesn't she at least deserve that? This will never end for us. Something has to be done to change the law to protect victims' rights. Despite everything, we're grateful to the police for finding Becky and letting us put her to rest. Had they followed procedure to the letter, my daughter could have lain in that field undiscovered for ever. We could have gone on for years, thinking she was still alive, hoping in vain that she'd come home one day. Given the choice, I would rather know. At the very least I could bring Becky home one last time and grieve for her, instead of clinging to false hopes.'

Karen's husband, Charlie, added: 'Tragically, nothing ever ran smoothly in Becky's short life and so it continues with her death. Our only comfort is that Halliwell is in prison and other young women are safe from him.'

They then revealed that at the age of just seventeen, Becky had been raped by a drug dealer and that they supported her and encouraged her to give evidence at his trial. After that, they tried repeatedly to help Becky, paying thousands of pounds for her to go into a private rehabilitation clinic. They took her to doctors, psychiatrists, counsellors and NHS drug treatment centres.

When Becky's father had left them, Karen thought the

children coped well with the split, but later she realised that Becky had been deeply traumatised. Then, when her father had a daughter with his new partner, Becky was jealous and felt further displaced from his affections. A shy girl just four feet eleven inches tall, she was bullied at school because her schoolmates found it unusual that she came from a single-parent household. Aged thirteen, she took an overdose and started self-harming, so eventually Karen took her out of school and educated her herself at home.

Things became more settled when Karen met Charlie. Becky got on well with him and was a delighted bridesmaid at their wedding in 1996. An intelligent girl, she wanted to go to university, so when she was sixteen Karen decided she should return to mainstream education. But her old s chool would not have her back and the local authority insisted that, given Becky's history, she should go to a special education centre.

'It wasn't long before I realised it was a school for dysfunctional teenagers who had trouble getting into mainstream schooling,' said Karen.

There, she fell in with a bad crowd.

'Looking back, I was incredibly naïve,' Karen told the *Mail*. 'Her new friends came from very troubled backgrounds, but I invited them to our home because I felt sorry for them and I wanted Becky to feel her new friends were welcome. But before long alcohol started to go missing from the house and I noticed money gone from my purse. When I asked Becky, she denied she had anything to do with it.'

One day, Karen was cleaning Becky's room and found a pile of aerosol cans under her bed. To her horror, she realised Becky was abusing solvents. Again, Becky denied everything.

When Karen tried to talk to her or suggest she seek help from the doctor, Becky would simply disappear. Often she would stay with her boyfriend and the eighteen-year-old lad she had met through her best friend at school.

Out of her mind with worry, Karen called social services, but they couldn't force Becky to return home because, at sixteen, she was no longer a child.

'Becky's psychiatrist told us that she had the emotional age of a twelve-year-old,' Karen said. 'She was like a child in a woman's body and other people took advantage of her. We faced one brick wall after another trying to get help for her.'

Eventually, Karen persuaded Becky to come home. By then, she had lost a lot of weight and suffered from violent mood swings, at times turning into a monster. The cause became plain when Karen found tin foil and other drugs paraphernalia in Becky's bedroom. Her daughter had been 'chasing the dragon' – that is, smoking heroin.

'When I confronted Becky, she burst into tears and told me, "Mum, my life is a complete mess, please help me,"' said Karen. 'She promised to stop and I tried everything to help her. I even phoned the police, but they just weren't interested.'

Karen and Charlie decided they had no option but to book her into a private drugs rehabilitation centre. But after they dropped her off, they were driving home when the clinic phoned and said: 'You need to come and collect her, she's causing trouble.'

'I replied, "She's a drug addict, what do you expect?" If they couldn't deal with her, how were we supposed to?' Charlie said.

Becky, despite short periods when she stayed off drugs, found it impossible to resist heroin and would simply run away.

'People always assume that druggies are from dysfunctional families, but it couldn't be further from the truth,' Karen told the *Sunday People*. 'Becky had everything a girl could want – a loving, supportive family who would do anything for her. She had her own bedroom with her own bathroom in a lovely house and she didn't want for anything, but nothing was more important to her than getting the next fix.'

Karen said she had lost count of the times she had received a phone call from Becky, after months of silence, telling her of yet another crisis and begging for her help. Karen would then go and fetch her daughter. Often she was filthy and lice-ridden, and Karen would have to nurse her back to health.

At one point, she even decided to buy heroin for her to try and wean her off.

'I knew that I was going to have to start providing this for her in order to keep her home and safe with me,' she said.

Karen regularly met dealers and would bury the drug in empty jam jars in the back garden.

'The last thing I needed was a police raid or Becky finding it,' she admitted. 'I had started to control the dosage and would slowly reduce it each time.'

Becky was jailed for three weeks after jumping bail over her involvement in a pub robbery. Karen last saw Becky on 17 December 2002. Becky had just been convicted for burglary and theft at Swindon Crown Court after admitting acting as a lookout for a drug dealer during a raid on a pub. Karen paid the fine and planned to drive Becky straight home. But Becky begged her mother to drive across Swindon so she could see her boyfriend, saying it would be 'just for half an hour'.

'I said, "Please, Becky, no," but she became more and more aggressive and hysterical, so I relented,' said Karen. 'I knew if I refused she'd run away again, so I drove her to this house and waited outside.'

After half an hour, Becky came out and begged her mother to let her stay for another half hour. Karen drove round the block. When she returned, Becky said, 'Please, Mum, I want to stay the night here.'

By then, Karen was in tears. She knew what was going on in that house. Becky was taking drugs again and Karen pleaded with her to come home. That was when Becky told her mother she was sorry, that she loved her and did not want to put her through hell any more and said she would come home when she was clean. Karen, Charlie and Steven regularly scoured the town looking for her, without success.

'Since Becky's remains were found, I keep thinking, "Would she be alive today if I'd insisted on driving her home?"' Karen told the *Mail*.

Even though Halliwell had led police to her body as well as Sian O'Callaghan's, he could not be charged on the basis of that implicit confession because, as already pointed out, Detective Superintendent Fulcher had not followed the correct procedure. At the time of Halliwell's arrest, he did not know Sian was dead, so he was leading an investigation into a possible abduction. Believing that Sian was still alive, he used an 'urgent interview' – usually deployed only in terrorism cases – to try to get Halliwell to reveal where she was so she could be rescued. This meant that Halliwell was not read his rights and his requests for legal representation were ignored.

After leading officers to Sian's body, Halliwell asked

Detective Superintendent Steve Fulcher for a cigarette in return for showing police 'another one', and took them to the field in Eastleach, where Becky was buried.

As he had not been cautioned, and legal representation denied, Halliwell's lawyers tried to have both murders dropped. Later, the judge ruled his rights had been breached so his confessions could not be used in evidence. However, there was enough forensic evidence in Sian's case for the prosecution to go ahead. But in Becky's case, there was not enough corroborating evidence to proceed. John Godden had lodged complaints with the Independent Police Complaints Commission and Fulcher had been suspended, though he received strong backing for his actions from both the O'Callaghan and Edwards families.

Karen was furious.

'Steve Fulcher was an incredible police officer,' she said. 'Let's not forget, without him we would not have discovered Becky's body. He's uncovered a serial killer. How can anyone punish him for that?'

But John Godden hit out at police, saying they had 'made massive mistakes'.

'It seems to me, "Come to Swindon, commit murder and you'll get away with it." That's the way I feel,' he said. 'I'll never put my trust in the police again. Why should we pay with this pain for somebody else's mistakes? I want proper closure. I want justice.'

Later he told *The Sun* that Halliwell must have had an accomplice. He insisted that the cabbie was too puny to hide Becky's body and must have had help. 'Police had to dig her up with mechanical diggers,' he said. 'There's no way he dug a hole that big on his own.'

And he had no sympathy for the detective everyone else thought was a hero.

'Fulcher should be bloody sacked,' Godden said. 'This was a hugely important conviction and police rushed it. There is still someone involved in that murder walking the streets.'

Becky's grandmother, Miranda Godden, said: 'Somebody murdered her, didn't they? Somebody's got to be punished. They can't just brush her under the carpet as though she was a nobody. She was a human being.'

Detective Chief Superintendent Pritchard assured Becky's relatives, saying: 'This very much remains a live investigation. I have a fresh senior investigating officer appointed to that inquiry and we will pursue all lines we can to secure justice for the family.'

Even Halliwell's younger sister, Sarah, was aghast that the second murder charge had been dropped.

'I can't believe he has got away with murder,' she said. 'I don't know what the police were doing. In his mind, he will think he has won. He's an evil bastard. He's done at least two murders. I can't believe he was doing nothing in that eight-year gap. But in his mind he will think he has got away with it. He'll think he's pulled the wool over the eyes of the judge, the police and everyone else. He'll be smirking in his prison cell tonight.'

She went on: 'He's playing games with the law, and with the families of his victims too. That's the unforgivable part. I think he should be strung up or shot. I wouldn't do it myself, but I think a life should mean a life and God knows how many lives he has taken or ruined. As it is, he should never ever be allowed out. He will always be dangerous because he is a completely cold fish. He doesn't relate to other people or care about them at all. I've had nothing to do with him since his arrest and I never want to see him or hear his name again. As a mum myself, it's Sian's parents I am thinking off, with another terrible Christmas for them coming up. My heart goes out to them.'

Later Becky's mother Karen Edwards said: 'I wish we could afford a private prosecution, I really do. But we've looked at the costs and it would bankrupt us. We don't know where to turn. We've got to live with this for the rest of our lives. Every day is a torment and more torture. The pain has been indescribable. Becky was such a beautiful girl – inside and out.'

CHAPTER TWELVE

THE TORMENT CONTINUES

Naturally, the strain of the case had taken a toll on Becky's mum Karen's health. She could not eat or sleep properly, and suffered fainting fits, panic attacks, chest pains, exhaustion and sudden surges of anger and paranoia. In her torment, she had driven hundreds of times past 'Becky's Field', where Halliwell buried her daughter three months before her twenty-first birthday in 2003.

Karen insisted the law must be changed to allow the prosecution of Halliwell.

'The lawyers originally told me this was a watertight case and he was going away for a very long time,' she said. 'Then I was told Halliwell would not be charged with Becky's murder – twenty minutes before going into court and seeing him face-to-face for the first time. It felt like someone had mashed my brain. My head was in a whirl. I just thought, "This can't be right." When I saw Halliwell in court I felt sick to the stomach. If they had let me at him he would never have walked out of there alive.'

She did not think that Halliwell was going to change his mind and own up.

'I don't think Christopher Halliwell has got any remorse,' she said. 'The justice system has let me down.'

Nevertheless, she sent a desperate letter to him in jail. In it, she said: 'I know you were responsible for the cruel and savage death of my only daughter Becky. My every waking moment is filled with the horrific thought of her terrifying, frightening moments as she suffered her death at your hands. The nightmare never ends. PLEASE could you find it in your heart as a father to tell us the truth about my beautiful girl. I am begging you please, admit Becky's murder.'

Karen said she was clinging to the slim hope that Halliwell would confess for the sake of his relationship with his own children.

'Remember you still have your daughters, it is time for you to start building bridges with your daughters,' she said. 'I can never replace my daughter but you could have the chance of getting yours back. Please don't prolong my suffering any longer, don't continue to taunt me after taking away the most precious gift in the world. I beg you again. Do the right thing and confess to Becky's murder.'

Halliwell did not respond.

With her husband Charlie, Karen made another visit to field where her daughter's body was found to lay a bouquet of pink roses and a decorative butterfly.

As she wiped away tears while she stood among nettles and thistles, she told the *Daily Mirror*: 'Look at it, it's so vast. I know what creeps me out – how many more bodies are in this field? He knew this place too well. Every time we've been out here we get lost. To think this was where Becky was all those years when we were out looking for her. I used to wake up at 1 a.m. and drive around searching for her, but I was looking for someone never to be found.'

She revealed that when Becky's body had been discovered, the skull and hands were missing. This could have been due to the field being ploughed, or it could have been a further attempt by Halliwell to hinder identification of the body. Fortunately, only one crop had been harvested since she was buried, so most of the corpse remained intact.

'To think her head is still out here somewhere in this field,' she said. 'Imagine burying your daughter without her head. He has taken away all her dignity. I still can't believe she is not here. I would give anything to have her back – anything. You know when you love something so much and it really hurts. It's just crucifying. Halliwell still has his daughters but I don't have mine. I'm just hoping that by sending him a letter in jail he will do the right thing by his daughters. No father wants to lose the love of his daughters and he needs to confess to Becky's murder for their sakes as well as mine. I'm begging him to confess, as a mother – and him as a father. My children are my life and always have been. It's just horrendous.'

Karen also told the *Mirror* how she met Halliwell's daughters, Natasha and Carissa, at Bristol Crown Court shortly before their dad was jailed the previous week.

'I hugged Natasha in the public gallery,' she said. 'She was sitting behind us listening to all the details of what her father did. She was broken-hearted. I said, "This is not your fault. You didn't do this. You are not to blame." She thanked me with a smile because they need kindness. They were both devastated and I have nothing but sympathy for them. They have lost their dad and I have lost my daughter.

'I don't blame Halliwell's family. They are victims in all this. He has affected so many lives. None of us will ever be the same again.'

It was Karen's first visit to the field since Halliwell was jailed.

'The farmer has been wonderful,' she said. 'He had the field blessed and is letting us plant an apple tree in Becky's memory. We themed Becky's funeral on pink – one of her favourite colours – and butterflies, which are very spiritual.'

Halliwell's daughter Natasha has also urged her dad to tell the truth about Becky's death. She said on ITV's *Daybreak* the day before: 'He needs to give the other family closure as well and give them the justice they need for their daughter.'

Carissa wrote to her father again, saying: 'You've confessed before, why not confess again?'

She explained: 'I knew someone had to do something to try to convince him, someone he loves. So without telling my mum or anyone, I sat down and wrote him a letter. I said to him that the court case was the hardest thing I've ever had to do. I told him we'd sat thirty centimetres from Becky's family in court and saw and heard their pain, and felt their pain to our cores. I said to him that he'd confessed before, so why not confess again but this time make sure it stood up legally.

'He'll be in prison for twenty-five years anyway, so why not end the agony for Becky's family? I also said in the letter that I want him in my life but that I can't have him in my life while he is still hiding things. The only way I can have any sort of relationship with him is if he confesses to everything and ends the agony for Becky's family. I said to him that if someone had harmed one of us, he'd have gone mad and that he'd want justice. I asked him to imagine the situation the other way around.'

She added that seeing Becky's mother and grandmother weeping in the public gallery at Bristol Crown Court was almost impossible to bear.

'Becky's mum was distraught and kept saying things like, "This isn't going to bring Becky back." Next to her was her mother, Becky's granny, who was just sobbing,' Carissa said. 'It was almost harder for me to see Becky's family than it was to hear, for the first time, the reality of what my dad had done. My sister and I were in tears seeing their pain.'

Halliwell's family were shocked when they found out in court he could not be tried for Becky's murder because of the mistake made by Detective Superintendent Fulcher.

'I hadn't understood the legal technicality and the scale of the police errors that meant that he was going to completely get off for Becky's murder and the Goddens wouldn't be getting justice,' said Carissa. 'I can't get the haunting images of the family's distress out of my mind. I can't move on until my dad does the right thing and makes a legal confession. I have no idea what his response will be but I hope he will listen to me.'

Halliwell wrote to relatives promising that as long as they asked him to his face he would tell them about anything 'you need me to answer'. It was a promise that he would not fulfil.

Becky's mother had already asked to see Halliwell so she could ask him to confess.

'This is something I'd never dream of doing in a million years, but I must battle on for Becky's sake,' she said. 'People ask: "Do you think you'd be able to do that?" It's not a question of wanting to. It's something I have to do if he'll see me. I need answers and he is the only person who can help me.'

The family were having a black headstone with hearts and angels made for Becky's grave at a cemetery in Swindon, but Karen has been unable to complete the inscription because she still did not know the date her daughter died.

'I asked the police if I could see Halliwell before he was sentenced and I asked again this week,' she told the *Daily Mirror*. 'They said, "He'd have to agree to see you." I'm still waiting for an answer. After years of torment I want to know when he murdered Becky so I can put a date on the headstone. I still haven't had a death certificate and I need a date for that too. I also need to know why he did it and I want to plead with him to admit it.

'I've seen him face-to-face in court and got over the initial shock. Meeting him in jail would be emotionally difficult but I'd do it for Becky's sake.'

She asked again for help from Halliwell's daughters: 'I would request of his daughters, please ask him to do the right thing.'

Meanwhile, the heartache was almost too much to bear.

'On days I feel weak my husband Charlie makes me strong again,' said Karen. 'He told me today, "Becky would be proud of you."'

With Halliwell convicted of the murder of Sian O'Callaghan and Becky Godden's murder still on the books, people began asking if Halliwell had killed other women.

A police source told the *Daily Mirror* that police wanted to know if there had been other victims. 'We have no doubt that, had he not been arrested for Sian's murder, he would have gone on to attack more women. From his teens onwards, we are looking at a potential offending period of more than thirty years. In the interests of truth and justice as well as compassion towards the loved ones of victims who will never return – we hope he will now tell us what he knows.'

Investigations were not confined to the Swindon area.

'We know he travelled all over the country working as a driver, or in the construction industry, and we are also looking at where he took his holidays on his narrow boat,' which he kept on the Kennet and Avon Canal, the *Mirror* was told. 'He could have left victims all over the UK. There is evidence from the way he disposed of Becky's body, with all clothing and jewellery removed, that he was very forensically aware. Books on forensics were found in his loft.'

Why did he change his car regularly, owning more than eighty cars during his career as a cabbie? Did his job as a taxi driver give him the opportunity to commit other offences? And he was a cunning criminal. Almost no evidence of his 'forensic footprint' could be found at the home he shared with his lover.

'There was very little sign of his presence,' the source said. 'It was as if he didn't live there. It leads us to ask if he has some other premises which contains his life and, horrifically, maybe trophies of his victims.'

It was then revealed that, when serving four years for stealing antiques from a country house in 1984, the twenty-year-old Halliwell had asked his cellmate Ernest Springer in HMP Dartmoor: 'How many women do you have kill to be a serial killer?'

'At least three,' said Springer, a career criminal from London's East End.

Halliwell then asked, chillingly: 'Have you ever thought of strangling your girlfriend during sex?'

A dossier on Halliwell was then passed to the serious crime analysis experts at the National Police Improvement Agency to see if they could link him to any historic unsolved crimes. No link was ever found.

CHAPTER THIRTEEN

THE CASE AGAINST THE DETECTIVE

Following the Sian O'Callaghan case, the Independent Police Complaints Commission (IPCC) issued a statement saying it was to independently investigate breaches of the 1984 Police and Criminal Evidence Act in the investigation into the deaths of Becky Godden and Sian O'Callaghan.

IPCC commissioner Naseem Malik said: 'Now that the criminal process has concluded, the IPCC can start its investigation into the police investigation into the tragic deaths of these two young women. We were unable to start work before criminal proceedings concluded on the advice of the Crown Prosecution Service. I have no doubt that there will be considerable interest in the circumstances that led to the IPCC investigations, but I would urge patience while we find out what happened.

'The IPCC has already concluded an independent investigation into five complaints against Wiltshire Police relating to the actions of the police during the investigation. Three of these complaints were upheld and the force has agreed our recommendation to offer the complainant an apology. The force has also confirmed to the IPCC that it has accepted our recommendation that it reviews its family liaison policy.'

The three complaints upheld referred to the police not informing the relatives of a press conference concerning Becky Godden and referring to her as Godden-Edwards.

The statement continued: 'The IPCC will also separately investigate allegations that Detective Superintendent Steve Fulcher from Wiltshire Police spoke about the case to some media outlets on separate occasions contrary to force instructions, the force media strategy and policies.'

Mr Latham had argued that his client could not receive a fair trial because, after Halliwell had led Fulcher to the bodies, the police officer said on live television that this was what had happened. The QC said it was bizarre that Fulcher had put information into the public domain that should in the normal course of things have been heard first by a jury. He argued the fact the suspect had led the police to the bodies would be 'engraved on the consciousness of the average juror', even though the prosecution were not allowed to mention these facts in the courtroom.

Fulcher's response was that he had had little sleep during the five days the police had searched for Sian O'Callaghan, then thought to be a kidnap victim. Although Halliwell had been under surveillance, he had not led them to her. When, finally, he had been arrested, Fulcher's only hope was that he would confess. But when he snatched up the phone to speak to the arresting officers, he learned that Halliwell had refused to comment. Fulcher then he took the momentous decision to order Halliwell to be taken to an isolated hilltop, where he took personal charge of the questioning.

There was pressure on Fulcher for some days. The police already had Halliwell in their sights. The day before his arrest, he had been interviewed by the police. It was noted that he had been close to tears but officers assured him that all local taxi drivers were being questioned. Then Fulcher used the media to turn up the heat, releasing a cryptic press release saying he was 'very close to identifying Sian's whereabouts'. He was hoping Halliwell would return to Sian, but then Halliwell was seen dumping a car seat cover and headrest in an industrial bin.

Fulcher had been awake all night worrying that Halliwell might kill himself before he could give up the secret of Sian's whereabouts. Nevertheless, he continued to let him run, under the watchful eyes of surveillance teams, in case he led to her. But when Halliwell headed to Boots to buy a big enough stash of paracetamol to kill himself, Fulcher was forced to send his troops in. Halliwell was cornered outside Asda as he was picking up a fare and was wrestled to the ground.

Fulcher had a pre-arranged plan. Officers carried out an 'urgent interview' in a blacked-out police car under clause C.11.1 of PACE, asking him where he was hiding Sian so that they could rescue her, but he refused to answer. They were allowed to do this without a solicitor present if they thought this could save the life of Sian. These were methods normally reserved for terrorist suspects – but under the grilling, Halliwell stayed silent, though detectives described him as looking 'like a rabbit caught in the headlights'.

When he revealed nothing, the officers decided to take him

to the station. But Fulcher ordered them to take Halliwell to Barbury Castle, the site of an Iron Age hill fort and local beauty spot popular with walkers and horse riders. Fulcher admitted that he had done so despite the reservations of his deputy. It was, he said later in court, the last opportunity he would have with Halliwell to 'look him in the eye and to ask him this one thing – will you take me to Sian?'

Fulcher said he believed she might be hidden nearby. He did not read Halliwell his rights nor allow him the lawyer he asked for. Fulcher believed he had no choice. He told a pre-trial hearing: 'On the one hand, I was cognisant of Mr Halliwell's rights. But my primary duty was to save Sian's life. My view was, there was an equation to balance between Mr Halliwell's right to silence and Sian O'Callaghan's right to life. My view was that Sian's right to life took a prior claim.'

It was a dilemma.

'My fear was, she could be dead; I hoped she was alive,' he said. 'My duty was clear: to work to find and protect Sian if I could. It's what any parent would have wanted a police officer to do for Sian.'

A cavalcade of police vehicles gathered at the beauty spot. Accompanied only by a civilian notetaker, Debbie Peach, Fulcher led Halliwell fifty yards from the police cars and conducted a nine-minute interview. Debbie's notes were later entered into evidence, though Fulcher had not cautioned Halliwell or offered him a solicitor, nor had Halliwell confessed to where Sian O'Callaghan was. However, the accuracy of the notes was not disputed.

FULCHER: 'Are you going to tell me where Sian is?'
HALLIWELL: 'I don't know anything.'

FULCHER: 'Are you going to show me where Sian is? What's going to happen. If you tell us where Sian is – that whatever you will be portrayed – you would have done the right thing.'

HALLIWELL: 'I want to go to the station.'

FULCHER: 'Are you prepared to tell me where Sian is?'

HALLIWELL: 'You think I did it.'

FULCHER: 'I know you did it.'

HALLIWELL: 'Can I go to the station?'

FULCHER: 'You can go to the station. What will happen is that you will be vilified. If you tell me where Sian is you would have done the right thing.'

The high-profile murder of Joanna Yeates in Bristol four months earlier and the smearing of Christopher Jefferies, who had only just been cleared, were still fresh in the memory.

HALLIWELL: 'I want to speak to a solicitor.'

FULCHER: 'You are being given an opportunity to tell me where Sian is. In one hour's time you will be in the press.'

HALLIWELL: 'I want to speak to a solicitor.'

FULCHER: 'You will speak to a solicitor. I'm giving you an opportunity to tell me where Sian is. By the end of this cycle you will be vilified, tell me where Sian is.'

HALLIWELL: 'Have you got a car? We'll go.'

Fulcher and Halliwell continued to talk in the back of a police car for forty-five minutes until they reached Uffington. Halliwell gave directions to a country road where he left Sian in undergrowth. By then, it was clear that Sian was dead, but Halliwell could not immediately pinpoint where he had dumped her body. However, he gave enough information for specialist search teams to find her at the bottom of a steep bank later that afternoon.

Still without cautioning him, Fulcher told Halliwell that confessing would be 'the right thing to do' for Sian and for Halliwell's family. He did not remind Halliwell of his rights, and it all came spilling out. Halliwell confessed that he had killed Sian by stabbing her in the base of her head. But he insisted he had not had sex with her.

'It appeared a weight was lifting from his shoulders,' said Fulcher.

The search team found Sian's body an hour later. She had been stabbed in the head and neck. She was lying face down and half-naked. Her bra had been torn off and underwear tampered with. Sections of cloth had been cut from her leggings and underwear.

At this point, when Detective Superintendent Fulcher was about to order that Halliwell be taken to the police station, the suspect told him: 'You and me need to have a chat.'

They drove a short distance, then got out of the car and sat down together on a grass bank and had a cigarette. According to Fulcher, they had developed a rapport and he wanted to keep Halliwell talking. Halliwell obliged, saying that he was a 'sick f***er', and asked the detective: 'Do you want another one?'

Again, Fulcher had failed to caution Halliwell or to furnish him with the lawyer he had asked for, fearing it might destroy the bond they had developed.

'It was the only chance to find out what he wanted to

show me,' Fulcher explained. 'No murder detective is going to abandon that line.'

Although he had solved two murders, only one case could be prosecuted as the only evidence in Becky Godden's case depended on an illegal interview. And Halliwell sought to cheat justice in the O'Callaghan case because of the way Fulcher had interviewed him.

Halliwell's barrister, Richard Latham QC, said that Fulcher showed an 'amazing contempt of all the recognised codes, rules and sub judice principles'. He insisted the PACE rules were a 'fundamental right' and suggested that Fulcher had 'gone back to the seventies style of policing'. His client had only confessed because Fulcher had resorted to 'good old-fashioned threatening conduct'.

Mrs Justice Cox agreed. She said Fulcher's actions were wholesale and irrefutable breaches of PACE. It had been a deliberate decision by Fulcher to carry out significant and substantial breaches of the code.

Questioning Halliwell on the hilltop had put additional pressure on him and could be seen as a mechanism to deny him his rights to legal advice, the judge said. She ruled out the fact that Halliwell had led Fulcher to the body of Sian O'Callaghan and that of Becky Godden, and ordered that any admissions he made during his four hours with Fulcher must not be put before a jury.

But Fulcher insisted that he had not put undue pressure on Halliwell. His confession had been entirely voluntary. As they drove the thirty miles to south Gloucestershire, Halliwell had said reflectively: 'Normal people don't go round killing each other.'

Once there, Halliwell pointed to an area in a forty-acre

field where he said he had buried another woman between 2003 and 2005.

'He took me to the exact spot by placing one foot in front of another after feeling a dip in the soil,' Fulcher said later. 'I gleaned we were going to find another murder victim. For three days afterwards we couldn't find a body. Then Becky's body was found a few metres from where Halliwell said it would be.'

Four hours after he had been arrested, Halliwell finally arrived at the police station. After that, on the advice of his solicitor and as Fulcher had predicted, he declined to make any further comment.

For the moment, Fulcher was Wiltshire Police's man of the hour – or 'flavour of the month', as he put it. He was even nominated for the Queen's Police Medal – the highest award in policing – for his work in extracting the killer's confession. This was a welcome accolade, as Fulcher was a career cop. He had a degree in criminology from Cambridge University. In 1986, he had joined Sussex Police, moving to Wiltshire in 2003. He had vast experience in major and serious organised crime, having held the position of Director of Intelligence and Head of Crime Investigation. As a senior investigating officer, he had been in charge of a number of high-profile murder investigations. After the successful hunt for Sian O'Callaghan's killer, he was seconded to the National Police Improvement Agency as a homicide expert and to the Serious Organised Crime Agency as regional adviser within Crime Operational Support. Fulcher returned to Wiltshire Police, only to be suspended while under investigation.

Other officers also lent their support. Colin Sutton, a former detective chief inspector with the Metropolitan

Police, told *The Daily Telegraph* that Fulcher had acted in a manner befitting a senior investigating officer by finding the bodies and bringing a sense of closure to the families of the two victims.

'He made a judgment in a dynamic and fast-moving situation and discovered the whereabouts of a missing person,' said Sutton. 'It was a reasonable decision and one an SIO should be able to make without fear of being second-guessed and suspended. As a result of his disciplinary action, SIOs might now think twice before taking that risk, and choose instead to preserve their own careers, which is a worrying and dangerous precedent.'

Keith Vaz MP, then the chairman of the Commons home affairs committee, said it could be an appropriate time to reform the Police and Criminal Evidence Act.

'We should never be in a position where regulations prevent people being brought to justice,' he said. 'The Act was fashioned almost thirty years ago and policing has changed enormously since then. Of course we need regulations and rules concerning how people are interviewed and also we need to recognise that policing has changed.'

He also express concern about the fate of Detective Superintendent Fulcher, saying it was regrettable that someone who had brought a murderer to justice had found himself embroiled in difficulties concerning the code of practice under the Act and he was sure the committee would want to review its procedures during its current inquiry into the IPCC.

The Labour MP was joined by Tory MP David Davies, among others calling for a change in the law.

'At the moment the Act stacks the odds in favour of the

offender,' he said. 'The case of this officer who tracked down a murderer and found two bodies is only the most serious example. It must be right that where a suspect volunteers extra information, the police are able to act on it.'

However, the Home Office insisted that the 1984 Police and Criminal Evidence Act, which was introduced after concerns about police conduct in several miscarriages of justice, including the case of the Birmingham Six, was an essential safeguard for suspects. The Association of Chief Police Officers agreed. It said: 'We need to work within the law, not above the law.'

Steve Williams, chairman of the Police Federation concurred: 'We have got to work within the confines of the law but sometimes the rules and regulations can tie our hands. Some of them do seem to favour the suspect. At a time of heavy cuts the police are finding it frustrating that they cannot provide the service the public deserves. They are under immense pressure and there may be a temptation to take shortcuts. Currently, morale among police officers is at rock bottom.'

The Police Superintendents' Association had provided legal support to Detective Superintendent Fulcher, who had been regarded as one of Wiltshire's finest detectives. Derek Barnett, the association's president, said that in fast-moving investigations the safety of a victim was paramount.

'Sometimes senior officers are faced with a dilemma of taking action that may save a life, or rigid adherence to policy or procedures,' he said. 'I think the public would expect police officers to exercise their discretion and professional judgment in a way that would prioritise the protection of life as the first and foremost consideration.'

THE CASE AGAINST THE DETECTIVE

Sean O'Neill, the crime editor of *The Times*, commented: 'This was not *Life on Mars* policing; there is no evidence of brutality or coercion. Mr Fulcher acted in the interests of the victims and their families. That was his downfall: he is now suspended, under investigation and looking at the end of his career... My path into journalism was shaped by cases such as the Birmingham Six – miscarriages that led to stringent safeguards for suspects and defendants. I still report on appalling police misconduct and corruption. But the concern should always be the pursuit of justice – for victims of crime as well as victims of abuse of police power – not the rulebook. Will justice be served if Mr Fulcher is drummed out of policing and Halliwell never faces trial for Becky's murder?'

Even Mrs Justice Cox admitted: 'It was not suggested that Detective Superintendent Fulcher's questioning was abrasive or aggressive.'

Fulcher himself outlined his dilemma, which concerned the fate of Sian O'Callaghan. 'My fear was, she could be dead; I hoped she was alive,' he said. 'My duty was clear: to work to find and protect Sian if I could. It's what any parent would have wanted a police officer to do.'

A police spokesman agreed: 'Is Fulcher a hero or a villain? The fact is, as soon as Halliwell was read his rights in custody, he did clam up. So if he'd been taken back to the station in the first place, they probably would never have found either body. On a human level, what Fulcher did was right.'

Even though the action Fulcher had been condemned for had prevented Halliwell being prosecuted for the murder of Rebecca Godden, her mother also rallied to his defence. 'Steve Fulcher is one in a million and deserves an MBE,' Karen Edwards insisted. 'Without him I would not have found my Becky. Steve has been the hero in all this. That man found my daughter and now he is being punished for it. It should be Halliwell who is being punished – not Steve Fulcher. It's just not fair. The law needs changing. I think it's absolutely disgusting.'

She asked for him to be cleared of any wrongdoing: the police need more flexibility when they're making arrests. There should be more policemen like Steve Fulcher. the world would be a better place and the streets safer.

'I have nothing but admiration for him and feel the law should be a bit more flexible to protect victims. If he had not acted the way he did we would never have known Becky was gone and I would always have had the false hope, the paranoia. Knowing is better than that. If he had played by the book, Halliwell would have been taken back to the police station with a lawyer and would have never said a word about where Becky and Sian's bodies were.

'Two families would have been left not knowing what had happened to their loved ones. How can what Steve Fulcher did be wrong? We are permanently living in a nanny state where it is all about the human rights of those people who commit crimes.'

She also told the *Sunday People* that if Detective Superintendent Fulcher had stuck to the rules they would never have even known that Becky was dead: 'I know for a fact that if Halliwell had been given a lawyer he would not have told the police where my Becky was buried. We may never have found her if it wasn't done this way.'

She aimed to get 100,000 signatures for a petition that called for a review of the Police and Criminal Evidence Act.

'I think a senior police officer should be able to make

decisions about the arrest at the time,' she said. 'Steve made a split-second one and the consequence is that he has now been suspended. It's very frustrating. Halliwell admitted in great detail that he had murdered my daughter. He even counted out his steps to show police where he had hid Becky's body in a remote field in the middle of nowhere. I fully support Steve and think he should be reinstated immediately and I wish there were more police officers like him. If it was not for him, Halliwell could still be driving around in a taxi and God only knows how many others there could have been.'

Even the holiday season did not lighten her mood – or stem her determination. 'Christmas has been horrendous and I just want all these celebrations to be over,' she said. 'My New Year is about campaigning for Becky and a change in the law. It makes my blood boil to think that Halliwell has got away with it, but I will never give up fighting for justice for Becky.'

Her MP, Robert Buckland, who was also a barrister, said: 'In the heat of a very charged atmosphere this policeman was doing his job. He was acting in good faith and we have to judge him in that context. He is not some dodgy copper such as Gene Hunt from the TV series *Life on Mars*. The codes of PACE are there for a reason but they are not set in stone and I believe there should be a review.'

Fulcher received further support from Tom Sebastiano, whose mother was murdered in Wiltshire in 2009. He said that Detective Superintendent Fulcher acted above and beyond the call of duty to support his family and convict his mother's killer.

'The idea that his skills are going to be lost simply because the rules are not fit for purpose is simply outrageous,' he said. 'Nobody seems to care about the rights of victims.'

Despite the general disquiet that Halliwell had not been prosecuted for the murder of Becky Godden – and thereby attracting a whole-life tariff – on 14 December 2012, the appeal court ruled against an attempt to increase the minimum jail term to be served by him. The three judges ruled the twenty-five-year tariff was not unduly lenient. Lord Justice Pitchford said they could see nothing amiss with the sentencing judge's reasoning when she set the minimum term.

CHAPTER FOURTEEN

NEAREST AND DEAREST

With Halliwell out of harm's way, the women in his life began to speak out, giving a searing insight into his psychology. The day after he was convicted, his partner Heather Widdowson gave her first press interview. She told *The Sun* that, only hours after he had murdered Sian O'Callaghan, they had had sex.

'He took me to bed that afternoon just hours after he killed her,' the fifty-five-year-old said. 'I don't know how he managed to keep his feelings to himself but I remember he was laughing and joking. He was completely normal. It felt like any other time we'd had sex. How could he do that? I'm repulsed to hear what he did to Sian. In all the time we were together he never showed any anger towards me. It never crossed my mind that he was capable of hurting me. Who knows what could have happened. It sends a shiver down my spine.'

She recalled the events of that night. 'Chris went to work early,' she said. 'It was a Friday. About 1.30 a.m., I sent him a text to see how he was doing. He said business was good and I got ready for bed. He texted again at 1.45 a.m. saying: "I love you." Next day he was up early and went to the car wash.'

It was unusual for him to get up so early, but he said he had to do a lot before going to the car. She did not realise that this would entail scrubbing Sian's blood off the car seats.

'I went to the shops and bought some tiles for the bathroom,' she said. 'He was gone for ages. When he came home, I joked: "If you do a bit in the bathroom, we can spend an hour in bed." When I turned around he was already under the duvet. I laughed and jumped in with him. Later I joked about ending the relationship but I wasn't being serious – I liked to say things to shake him up a bit. But at dinner time he was off his food and he went to work early.'

Like everyone else in Swindon, Heather was concerned about the disappearance of Sian. Halliwell feigned concern too, she recalled with distaste, putting posters of the appeal in his car. Then the police came around to the house they had shared in Ashbury Avenue since 2003, saying that they were interviewing all cabbies in the area. Nothing seemed amiss, at first.

'Chris seemed relaxed,' Heather said. 'But the officer took out a DNA test and I watched the colour drain from Chris's face. He looked reluctant when he gave a sample, but he'd been in trouble in the past, and I put his worries down to that. After the police left I asked if he was in the area where Sian went missing. He said "no".'

The next morning, at 7 a.m., Heather returned from her the night shift at a medical firm to find Halliwell awake in bed.

'He seemed distracted and not his usual self,' she said. 'He kept telling me he loved me. It didn't feel right. His behaviour was out of character.'

She went to bed and, at 11 a.m., she was woken when the police came around again. This time they brought the news that Halliwell had been arrested for murder.

'I fell apart,' she said. 'I couldn't believe what they were telling me. At the station they said there was no doubt he'd done it. I showed them the text messages. It was then I realised an hour after saying he loved me he'd taken someone's life. I'll never forgive him for what he has done.'

In an instant, she found her life in tatters.

'I couldn't go home,' she said. 'The house that I'd had for twenty years was now a crime scene. I went to my friend's and slept on her sofa. In one day I'd lost everything.'

Things got worse when, the following day, the police revealed that Halliwell had also led them to the body of Becky Godden, who had disappeared around the time they had met.

'In all the years I'd been with Chris, he was hiding this sick secret,' Heather said. 'I wondered if I'd ever really known him.'

Heather had met the cabbie in 2003 and they moved in together when he split with his wife.

'We had a happy, loving relationship,' said Heather. 'We both worked odd shift patterns but managed to find time for each other. He was quiet and normally kept his feelings to himself but he once told me he'd done "horrendous" things when he was young. But I didn't want to know what. I knew he'd been in prison and had a difficult childhood. He was beaten by his mum from the age of three and left home at sixteen. But now I know he's a sick man. I don't know why he did it. He had a good life. There was no reason for him to do it.'

Her heart went out to the families of his victims.

'Sian and Becky were just innocent young girls,' she said. 'They trusted him. As a taxi driver, he was supposed to keep them safe. I've no feelings for Chris now. He is a cold, callous coward and I'll never forgive him for what he has done.'

She also revealed that he had showed her the murder weapon – a kitchen knife with a six-inch blade – just days before the murder. 'He said it was for self-defence,' she recalled.

Halliwell's ex-wife Lisa, a nurse, also spoke to the press. She said that the killer was similarly untroubled when he collected his teenage son in his taxi the day after he raped and murdered Sian. She also said he later sent a grovelling letter to his family, begging their forgiveness.

His daughter Natasha went on ITV's *Daybreak*, saying that he should do the right thing and tell the truth over the murder of Becky Godden.

'He needs to give the other family closure as well and give them the justice they need for their daughter,' she said.

Asked whether her father ever explained to her what he did when she visited him in jail, she said: 'No, never. He said to me, because I saw him, he said, "Don't ask me why because I don't know why." So I don't think he even has an explanation.'

Halliwell had written to her several times, advising her to change her name. Other members of the family had also received letters from him, but had not replied.

'We have had quite a few letters that have said, "Sorry for putting you all through this" and things like this,' Natasha said. 'As much as I want to hate him, I can't. I pity him and I do feel sorry for him and I hate what he has done but I can't hate him.'

Halliwell's sister Sarah said she had always loathed Halliwell and told how he 'did strange things showing no emotion' as they grew up together. He had a strange disturbing aura about him and cold blue eyes 'like chips of ice'.

'He was just not a normal child,' she explained. 'I have witnessed things he did at first hand – and it was very unpleasant. He loved trapping spiders and butterflies and taking his time to pull off their legs and wings one by one. It was like a hobby to him and he showed no emotion while he was doing it. He would just smile as these creatures struggled and finally died. He has always lived in a strange world of his own.'

Sarah was two years younger than her brother and suffered at his hands.

'Things happened between Chris and I that I will never forgive him for. I hate him,' she said.

Their childhood had not been easy. The two children were subjected to cruel discipline at the hands of their stepfather. They were regularly beaten with a leather strap or dragged out of bed and hit in the middle of the night. Halliwell soaked up the beatings, but he grew to loathe his mother and got his own back by doing vile things.

'He is a very cold, detached person who could never handle normal relationships,' said Sarah. 'If ever you had a go at him he would just stare you out with those vile eyes and say nothing.'

Halliwell went to school in Dalbeattie, Kirkcudbrightshire, and spent a summer working in a butcher's shop in the town. Former colleagues at the shop, Carson's, remembered working with him.

Norman Neilson said: 'My brother and I worked in the same shop and we remember this quiet, thin young boy. He did the sweeping up and cleaning, as well as basic butchering tasks. It was around the time he left school and he was only about sixteen.'

By then their mother, who died in 2009 at the age of sixty-five, had finally had enough of Halliwell and got shot of him. When he was fifteen, she dumped him on a foster family.

'I will never forget the way it was done,' Sarah said. 'We drove Chris to some council place and left him in a room for the foster people to pick him up. Then my mum and stepdad just drove home without saying a word. There were no tears from Chris at being kicked out of his own family. He just stared straight ahead. He told me he hated Mum and had no feelings for her. The truth is my mother was a cruel woman and what she did affected me and my brother.'

That cruelty rubbed off on Halliwell, as Sarah discovered when she went to lodge with him and his wife in Swindon.

'I found out I was pregnant with my first child and thought Chris and Lisa would be pleased for me and help me,' she said. 'But he just told me, "Get out" straight away, packed my bags and left them in the hall. I told him I would be pregnant and homeless but he just said, "Cheerio".'

Despite her brother's rebuff, she kept in touch with Halliwell's children, especially her eldest niece, through Facebook. Natasha stayed with her in Stroud and confided that she only had sporadic contact with her dad, even though they lived in the same street.

'He only saw the children when it suited him,' Sarah said. 'He was never going to make a good dad with his background.'

The last time Sarah had seen her brother was at a family reunion at a McDonald's in Swindon.

'He hadn't changed a bit,' she said. 'He was still as cold as ice and still had that awful stare. Now all I can think about is what the families of those two dead girls are going through.'

He was now behind bars and she was pleased.

Meanwhile, the people of Swindon were outraged by a publicity stunt undertaken by the bosses of the Suju nightclub, which was festooned in police hazard tape for their 'Haunted Horror House' Halloween event.

Local resident Sarah James said: 'I was driving past the nightclub when I saw what they were attempting to promote their Halloween event. It is a horrific, sick and tasteless PR attempt. The organisers are vulgar and should be ashamed of themselves for their actions. Sian was a much-loved member of the community and for Suju, the last place she was seen alive on CCTV, to do this is horrific. I know many people were outraged by what they did and I for one will be boycotting the nightclub from now on. It is disgusting.'

Hannah Strange was also horrified when she saw the display outside Suju.

'I was shocked to see all the tape across the club,' she said. 'I immediately thought a serious incident had taken place. When I heard it was just something about Halloween, I thought it was in poor taste, given her killer has only just been jailed.'

Another local, Kirstie Mills, added: 'I thought something bad had happened related to Sian O'Callaghan – it worried me a little bit. This is completely untactful after recent events.'

Pete Shawe, the partner of Sian's mother Elaine, said the club's management had some explaining to do. 'The police had been in touch as the manager of Suju has been upset at the reaction to it and wants to explain himself to us,' he said. 'I think it's in poor taste and thoughtless, I can't imagine they didn't think there would be a reaction. I can only guess their reasoning.'

A post on their Facebook page said: 'We would like to state that the tape has now gone from out Suju for another year.'

Memories of Becky would not lie down either, after her aunt, Tracey Mullane, discovered a ghoulish photograph in an album in the loft. It showed her at a wedding reception at Swindon's De Vere Hotel in 2008. In the crowd a few feet away from her is the man who murdered her niece some five years earlier – a smirking Chris Halliwell.

'After his arrest the groom's sister confided, "I've got something to tell you – Halliwell was at the wedding." I felt sick to the stomach because he looked so insignificant and acted normally throughout that day, seemingly without a care in the world, appearing as if nothing untoward had ever happened to him,' Tracey told the *Sunday Mirror*. 'But the odds against him being at a wedding with Becky's relatives must be a million-to-one, at least, and fall into the realms of coincidence and bad luck.'

Tracey said she was asked to confirm to police that Halliwell was in the picture. 'I told them he had an evil look about him, and now, of course, I know that's the case. He is evil,' she said. 'It was fortunate Becky's mum Karen, my sister, wasn't there. She and Becky's stepdad have suffered enough without unknowingly rubbing shoulders with Halliwell. It was a small, intimate wedding. None of us could believe that Halliwell passed himself off as a normal bloke. He's two people in one.'

Although there was no trial, an inquest into Becky Godden's death took place at Oxford Coroner's Court in April 2013. Delivering a narrative verdict, coroner Darren Salter said: 'On the available evidence, it is very likely her death was unnatural, violent and due to the unlawful actions of a third party.'

He said when her remains were found in a field in Eastleach, Gloucestershire, her head, arms and part of her feet were missing. She had last been seen, aged twenty, in Swindon in late 2002. Forensic pathologists used DNA to identify her, but were unable to determine how she had died. They found no trace of the missing bones and it was not known what happened to them.

'All I got back of her was a plastic bag of her bones – and no head,' said Becky's mother. This led to the theory that Halliwell may have gone back to the victim's grave later to chop off her head, hands and feet, an inquest heard. The coroner concluded she had died 'at an unknown location at the end of 2002 or the beginning of 2003'.

Detective Sergeant Peter Ritson told the hearing that a murder investigation into Becky Godden's death was continuing. Halliwell's name was not mention during the proceedings of the coroner's court. The Oxfordshire coroner said he had a 'limited remit' regarding the circumstances of Godden's death.

Speaking afterwards, Karen Edwards pleaded with Halliwell, saying: 'I would also like to appeal to Christopher Halliwell. This is your chance now, come clean, please, please, what have you got to lose? My personal opinion, I don't think he's ever going to come out, so why not put everyone out of their misery? There's only one person who knows what truly happened and we all know who that is. She is my daughter and I'm not going to give up. Until I get that conviction I will not rest. Every day is a day closer to getting that.'

She added: 'I feel that as her mum I will get to the root of this. Even if it's with the last breath in my body, I will get a conviction of some description.'

She also made a broader appeal for fresh evidence.

'What I would like to do is, anybody out there who knows anything at all – any tiny, tiny, little bit of evidence – anything that may help convict Becky's murderer,' she said. 'Any tiny little thing and I would be eternally grateful. Just please get in touch with the police. This is still very much an open murder investigation.'

By then, Detective Superintendent Fulcher's suspension had been lifted, although he was still awaiting the IPCC's report. Meanwhile, Wiltshire Police refused to say what he was doing.

'The police have a very hard job. I am delighted that Steve Fulcher is back at work,' said Karen Edwards. 'Without him I would never had known what happened to my daughter, whether she was alive or dead. I think he's a brilliant officer who didn't deserve reprimanding. He was doing the right thing as well as his duty. This has been a complete nightmare for us but he has been living that nightmare as well. For ten months he has been in limbo not knowing whether he can continue in the job that he has given his life to. Without Steve's actions we would never have found Becky's body and yet he has been punished.'

John Godden, who was also at the inquest, said: 'Becky

had a wonderful personality. She was the life and soul. All we want is justice.'

Afterwards, Karen again visited the field where Becky had been found to lay flowers.

'I avoid this place like the plague,' she said. 'But it was an important and meaningful gesture being here today. I don't want Becky feeling alone and abandoned.'

CHAPTER FIFTEEN

GROSS MISCONDUCT

Despite the plaudits of the families and other supporters, the Independent Police Complaints Commission found that Detective Superintendent Fulcher had a case to answer for gross misconduct.

'The effect of Detective Superintendent Fulcher's actions was catastrophic, particularly on the prosecution of Mr Halliwell for the murder of Rebecca,' the IPCC's report said when it was published on 8 September 2013. 'Detective Superintendent Fulcher stated had he not proceeded as he did, Rebecca's remains may never have been found. However, it is not possible to determine what may or may not have happened if Mr Halliwell had been immediately conveyed to custody after his arrest and urgent interview by detectives.'

IPCC Deputy Chair Rachel Cerfontyne added: 'This investigation has been a highly unusual one. We will never know what may have happened if the PACE codes had been followed.'

The IPCC report went on to say that PACE and its codes of practice were 'not optional', adding: 'They are a fundamental part of the criminal justice process and exist to ensure the rights of suspects, and therefore the integrity of the whole process, are protected.'

It also said that Fulcher should face disciplinary action for briefing the media on the case when he had been told not to.

'This is a difficult time for all concerned with this case and especially the families and friends of Sian and Becky, especially after all they have already had to endure,' Cerfontyne continued. 'We will never know what may have happened if the PACE codes had been followed. However, Detective Superintendent Fulcher's actions were in deliberate breach of PACE and we find that he has a case to answer for gross misconduct. Also, Detective Superintendent Fulcher, despite no longer having responsibility for Operation Mayan [the on-going murder investigation], and against express orders, went ahead with meetings about the case with journalists from both the BBC and ITV.'

The IPCC examined the information Fulcher gave to the media in the forty-eight hours after Halliwell's arrest and shock confession, as well as his conduct in granting television interviews in later months to local news reporters Steve Brodie and Rob Murphy, against the wishes of his superiors. The report said Fulcher was 'dishonest' and 'lacked integrity' in the way he disobeyed advice and orders not to do TV interviews.

The report outlined how, in the frantic twenty-four hours after Halliwell was initially arrested – with Sian O'Callaghan still missing – there was a major falling-out between Detective Superintendent Fulcher and the head of the police's media department, Steve Coxhead. The IPCC investigators said they did not understand why a press conference was hastily called at 5 p.m. that day, just hours after Halliwell had confessed to two murders, finally arrived at a police station and had access to a solicitor. Fulcher then told the media of the second confession, and the IPCC said it was worrying that a senior officer did not apparently realise that these matters were sub judice.

'This behaviour is even more extraordinary when set in the context that the trial judge had already considered whether force press conferences given by Detective Superintendent Fulcher were prejudicial to the case against Halliwell,' Cerfontyne said. 'We find that he has a case for gross misconduct for this as well and it will now be for Wiltshire Police to decide what action to take and I await their proposals.'

Becky's mother was furious with the report and accused the IPCC of putting the killer's rights above hers, stoutly defending Detective Superintendent Fulcher.

'He's my hero and should not be punished,' she said. 'He's accused of breaching Halliwell's rights, but what about mine? Don't they count for anything? Detective Superintendent Fulcher should be hailed as a hero, not as someone who overstepped the mark. The rules should be tailored to help us as much as an accused person. Without Detective Superintendent Fulcher's initiative I would never have had closure. Yes, sadly Becky is dead, but I could have spent the rest of my life wondering if she was still out there alive, simply not wanting to see me, or dead. Everyone I speak to is outraged. The PACE laws are rightly designed to protect the innocent, but now we are letting the criminals get away with murder.'

She insisted that Detective Superintendent Fulcher stay in

his post. 'He's a top detective with a degree in criminology and if he can't make a decision on a shout like this then we are living in a pretty poor country,' she said.

She went on to tell *Channel 4 News* that she backed Fulcher 'one hundred per cent', adding: 'I'm indebted to Steve Fulcher. He brought my little girl home. I wouldn't have been able to put her to rest had it not been for him, so why should he be punished?'

She also renewed her call for a public debate on PACE rules. However, John Godden's complaint that Fulcher's action had led to the charge against Halliwell for the murder of his daughter being dropped was upheld.

The Wiltshire police force said it would give careful consideration to the recommendations made over Fulcher's handling of the case.

'We are taking this matter very seriously and we are currently in the process of carefully considering the recommendations made within the report and our subsequent response to the IPCC,' said a spokeswoman. 'We will be taking into account the needs of the families whilst deliberating the recommendations. Wiltshire Police are continuing to offer welfare support to Detective Superintendent Fulcher throughout this ongoing process.'

Having reviewed the IPCC report, they decided that Fulcher's actions should be the subject of a formal conduct hearing.

'This is a complex and emotive matter that involves a number of parties,' the police said. 'We believe that it is important that this should be dealt with through the right process, fairly, independently and in an open and transparent manner. We are currently in the process of arranging the conduct hearing with an independent panel of senior officers from other forces so that due process can continue. Wiltshire Police are continuing to offer welfare support to Detective Superintendent Fulcher.'

Meanwhile, Minister of State for Policing and Criminal Justice Damien Green said a review of the guidelines was being looked at: 'It may be PACE needs to be changed, maybe not. I await to see the results of the various pieces of work on this before I can come to a proper conclusion.'

Karen Edwards' petition continued apace, though she risked her life gathering signatures among the raucous football crowd at a highly charge derby match between Swindon and Bristol City.

'It was my first football match experience, although I didn't watch the game,' she said. 'It was horrendous, to be honest. There were police dogs going mad, horses, bottles flying everywhere, running battles – it was like being in the middle of a riot and there was me and my friends with our little stand trying to get signatures. It was unbelievable, I found it diabolical, to be honest. I couldn't believe this was what football was like.

'I wasn't scared – when you've been through what I've been through, nothing scares me now. But I was worried for my ladies who are helping me, they all got split up in the mêlée and we couldn't find each other. But I still managed to get seven hundred signatures in just a few minutes, which was great. I went back on Tuesday night to the Chelsea match, and it was a completely different story – everyone was friendly, there was no trouble and they were queuing up to sign it.'

She said many Chelsea fans remembered the case and wanted to support her call for a review of the PACE rules. The campaign also called for Detective Superintendent Fulcher to keep his job. 'Without him, we wouldn't have found Sian O'Callaghan's body, and we would not have known what happened to Becky, let alone found her body,' she said. 'I've been in contact with the families of other murder victims on cases that Mr Fulcher dealt with and they all say he's a hero who solved their horrible cases.'

She had set up tables in supermarkets across Swindon to solicit signatures and also had an e-petition on the 'Justice for Becky' website. 'Steve Fulcher deserves a medal,' she said. 'I'm gutted to think the man who got my daughter back may lose his job, it's absolutely disgusting.'

Along with the petition, Karen amassed boxes of evidence concerning Becky's and other similar cases. They were stored, under lock and key, in her daughter's bedroom, just in case further charges could eventually be brought against Halliwell.

On 22 January 2014, Detective Superintendent Fulcher was brought before a formal conduct hearing. He faced the sack, but instead was given a final written warning. He admitted that he had not cautioned the killer: 'I believed that again, the right thing to do was take the information he was prepared to give, but I accept he was not cautioned at that time.'

In a statement released through his legal team, Fulcher said that he wanted to return to his job.

'Mr Fulcher wishes to express his thanks to those who have supported him throughout this very sad case,' said the joint statement from his lawyers and the Police Superintendents' Association. 'At all times Steve Fulcher has been motivated by a desire to serve the public and do the best that he can for the victims, their families and for Wiltshire Police.

GROSS MISCONDUCT

'He is grateful for the support he has received from many people and, in particular, humbled by the support he has received from Becky's mother, Karen Edwards, and Sian's partner Kevin Reape, when they have suffered such tragic loss. Steve Fulcher is a dedicated police officer and is fully committed to the Wiltshire Police. He wishes to return to work as soon as possible to continue serving the public and to move forward from this upsetting and stressful episode in his life and that of his family.'

Karen Edwards again spoke out in his defence, praising him for bring her 'little girl home': 'He has done over and above his call of duty and he is now being punished for it. He is a hero. How many police officers would have done what he did? How many would have put his job on the line and taken that risk? If it had been somebody else perhaps they would have stuck to PACE and ignored the fact there was another body, which had been confessed to, and that body would still be out there. PACE was put there to protect the innocent, now the guilty are getting away with murder because of it. We're the living example and proof of that. If Steve hadn't done what he did, we wouldn't have known about Becky. She would have still been lying there in that field and possibly Sian could have been there.'

She was overjoyed when she heard that he was going to keep his job.

Wiltshire Police Chief Constable Pat Geenty said in a statement: 'The panel have ruled that the appropriate sanction is for Detective Superintendent Fulcher to be issued a final written warning. Clearly, this case has been very emotive and has attracted a high level of public interest due to the tragic circumstances surrounding it. Serious and major crime investigations are a complex aspect of policing and are often fast-paced and highly charged. I have great admiration for senior investigating officers across the country who have to make life-and-death decisions.

'As always, it is vital that investigations are rigorously reviewed in order that good practice, lessons learnt and areas for development are identified. Furthermore, in line with the very prominent national concern regarding the integrity and transparency of the police service, I reiterate that I expect the highest level of professional conduct from all of my officers and staff. I fully respect the findings of the panel today and the process that has taken place, and I abide by the decision they have made.

'Detective Superintendent Steve Fulcher acknowledges and accepts the findings of the panel and is grateful for the thorough consideration given to the facts of his case. At all times Steve Fulcher has been motivated by a desire to serve the public and do the best that he can for the victims, their families and for Wiltshire Police.'

He was also found guilty on the second charge over his relationship with the media. 'The panel have upheld the allegation that Detective Superintendent Fulcher committed gross misconduct by breaching the standards of professional behaviour as outlined by the Police Conduct Regulations 2008,' Wiltshire Police said. 'The panel has decided the most appropriate action is for Detective Superintendent Fulcher to be given a final written warning. He will remain within Wiltshire Police.'

However, four months later, Steve Fulcher resigned from the force.

CHAPTER SIXTEEN

FRESH FINDS

On 10 April 2014, the police returned to Baxter's Farm after the farmer unearthed more human remains while ploughing near the original site. The police said that 'a bone, believed to be human', had been found in the vicinity of Becky's shallow grave. It was later found to belong to Becky.

The following month, one of Sian's boots was found in the River Kennet at Ramsbury, Wiltshire, twelve miles from Swindon. Another was found in a pond, along with a broken single-barrelled shotgun. Specialist divers pulled the boot from the muddy water just as reporters were arriving for a press conference. The police launched fresh searches for Sian's other missing possessions including her keys, handbag, mobile phone and items of jewellery, along with the knife Halliwell used to kill her.

The first boot had been found as the police scouted the area as part of the continuing investigation. Detective Chief

Inspector Sean Memory, who was leading the search, said: 'On Wednesday, myself and a colleague were doing some inquiries out in this area, looking for waterways that might be involved in Sian's murder. We noticed a shoe bobbing in the pond, we started to look at each other in amazement. We know Sian was missing a shoe, her boot, and some other property. I went to the local fire station, got a ten-foot pole and hooked the boot out, and we realised we had recovered the left boot belonging to Sian.'

It marked a significant advance in the investigation.

'This tells us Christopher Halliwell used this site as a deposition site,' said Memory. 'It offers a piece of the jigsaw as to what happened to Sian. I was able to say I am pretty sure Sian has been brought to this location. I can't say she was murdered here but I can tell her phone was here as well, so it would indicate this is a location she may well have been murdered at.'

Thirty officers from Wiltshire Police's Major Crime Investigation Team, along with dive teams and cadaver dogs from South Wales looking for a body, were now combing the area.

Detective Chief Inspector Memory added the find was bringing back a lot of memories for Sian's mother Elaine. 'She has not been able to get closure on her daughter's murder but she had tried to move on and I think this find is bringing a lot back,' he said. 'It was a difficult conversation to have because obviously Halliwell was convicted of Sian's murder two years ago. But I hope this helps to fill in gaps about what might have happened to her and where she may have been taken.'

The police had yet to speak to Halliwell about the finds. Memory said the police were still investigating Becky's murder: 'I can't rule anything out with what we will find at this location. Obviously it is significant and I'm really open-minded about what we might find here.'

They were also keeping an open mind about what else they might find and the pond where one of Sian's boots was found was to be drained.

'The specialist dive team from Avon and Somerset will continue their efforts at the scene tomorrow when they will drain the pond and conduct further searches,' a police spokeswoman said. 'Searches by police officers and cadaver dogs are also continuing. Hilldrop Lane remains closed and diversions are in place.'

The pond was eight feet deep and hundreds of gallons of water drained from it had to be sieved. The police would then undertake a fingertip search of the silt at the bottom and remained optimistic about the finds they might make in and around the pond.

'I am really open-minded about what we may find here over the next few days,' said Memory. 'What I will say is when we leave here we will recover every piece of evidence we are physically able to do. I am leading the Becky Godden investigation and we will recover everything we can and identify who that property belongs to, and I am very open-minded about that.'

Within days, some sixty pieces of women's clothing had been found buried in the woods nearby.

'Someone has made some effort to hide it,' said Memory. 'There are in excess of sixty items of material, such as a sleeve, a zip or a hood, so it is difficult to say exactly how many items of clothing there are.'

He did not know how long the clothing had been there,

but some of the items appeared to have been buried for some time. 'There may be a really innocent explanation and someone may have fly-tipped it,' he added. 'Equally it is really unusual to find women's clothing buried. It may genuinely have no significance at all but I am open-minded as to why someone would bury clothing. But to me it does seem a very strange location to be burying clothes, given what else we have found here.'

The police appealed for anyone who knew anything about why the clothes had been buried around a hundred yards from a pond in Ramsbury, so they could rule out any potential links to Halliwell.

A police spokeswoman said: 'The clothing has been taken away for examination. It includes a chunky knitted cardigan. At this stage there is nothing to link the items to any other crimes and it is possible it was left by a fly-tipper.'

The items were undergoing painstaking forensic tests as the police wanted to check if the clothing belonged to other missing women.

'We are satisfied that these clothes did not belong to Sian O'Callaghan,' Wiltshire Police said. 'Officers are keeping an open mind as to why they are there. Detectives are keeping an open mind around all of the findings and as to why the shotgun or clothing might be at the location.'

Of course, Becky's clothes had not been found.

'I am satisfied the clothing does not relate to Sian O'Callaghan,' said Memory. 'But I don't know what Becky Godden was wearing when she disappeared or exactly when she disappeared.'

Despite the intensive search, nothing else of significance was found. The police were particularly interested in the chunky-knit cardigan, which was found closer to the pond than the other items. Meanwhile, the labs were searching for traces of DNA.

'The forensics work on the items discovered there is very complicated and will take a number of weeks at least,' a spokesman said. 'All of the items found, including Sian's boots, shotgun, chunky-knit cardigan and pile of sixty items of material or clothes, have been sent for forensic analysis. This is likely to take several weeks.'

Speculation continued as to whether Halliwell had killed Sian at the site, or simply dumped her boots there later to dispose of the evidence. Her body was found ten miles away in Oxfordshire. Detectives were said to have the DNA of three other missing women, or close family matches to them, ready to compare with any samples found on the clothing. They were on the lookout particularly for strands of hair.

'We are being methodical and careful,' a CID officer told the *Sunday Express*. 'We don't want to make any mistakes and the major thrust is to find some link to Becky so we can re-interview Halliwell under caution. A buried cache of clothing is unlikely to be fly-tipping. There may be an innocent explanation, but everything hinges on the work of the forensic scientists. The discovery of Sian's boots, together with a shotgun barrel, in the pond nearby is undeniably sinister.'

The find gave the police renewed reasons to investigate whether Halliwell was a serial killer.

'Sian was picked up in the early hours of the morning outside a club in Swindon on March 19, 2011,' a source said, 'Sian, of course, did the right thing and got into a cab to take her home, a cab driven by the father of one of her friends at that. Halliwell has then driven her out of Swindon in his green Toyota Avensis and away from her home.'

Halliwell would have driven along the A4 into the Savernake Forest.

'We know from her mobile phone records that Sian was in the Savernake half an hour after she was picked up by Halliwell. What we now know is Halliwell must have then taken her out of the forest, across the A4, on to a narrow lane that winds down to join the road from Marlborough to Ramsbury. He probably took a left turn on to the Aldbourne road and then right on to Hilldrop Lane at the next junction. She may have died at Hilldrop but she was buried miles away at Uffington, on the other side of Swindon in the Vale of the White Horse.'

The woodland at Hilldrop, it was feared, may have been a killing ground.

'Hilldrop Lane is not an obvious spot, and it's fair to surmise Halliwell had been there before. If it turns out items of clothing at Hilldrop belong to more than one missing woman it would go towards confirming the rather chilling theory that he may have had a routine.'

Firearms experts examined the gun barrel found in the pond, which seemed to have had its stock removed.

On 31 May 2014, a spokeswoman for Wiltshire Police announced: 'The searches in the Ramsbury area have been completed as of 4.30 p.m. and the items found are now subject to review and testing. Detectives are in the early stages of the review and forensic testing. Wiltshire Police have made no links to the missing women mentioned or any other cases at this stage.'

She dismissed the comments of the *Sunday Express*'s informant. 'Although a CID source has been quoted, the comments made by this individual are highly speculative and unhelpful to our investigations,' she said. 'Detectives are in the early stages of the review and any forensic testing. Speculation such as this is unhelpful and can be potentially distressing for families who may have lost their loved ones. Wiltshire Police are committed to ensuring a thorough investigation and will maximise any evidential opportunities that are found. However, at this stage it is too early to make links to missing women or to speculate on why the items were found there.'

While Halliwell had not been charged, the investigation of the murder of Becky Godden continued. On 24 September 2014, detectives appealed for information on a silver Volvo in relation to the case. The following month, forensic officers made another search of Halliwell's former home, where he had lived his wife Lisa and their children. At the time of Halliwell's arrest it had only been given a small-scale search, the police said. The forensic investigation then had concentrated on the house six doors away, where he lived with Heather Widdowson. A forensic tent was put up again outside the semi-detached house and uniformed police stood guard. The new owners of the house were forced to move out while the floorboards were taken up and the loft space searched.

'We are focusing our attention on this property as part of the ongoing investigation and have organised a specialist team comprised of over thirty staff,' said Detective Chief Inspector Memory. 'I believe this house is involved in the murder of Becky Godden, and I am looking for any evidence that will link to Becky or to her murder. When I leave here I want to be sure we have done everything we possibly can, so I can say to her family that we have carried out a thorough search. These officers are concentrating their search for any items which may be related to Becky's murder or may assist with the investigation into her death.

'We have a number of crime scene investigators who will conduct meticulous fingertip searches of the property. This will include the removal of flooring, exploring space behind walls and in loft areas and a methodical search carried out until I am satisfied that the entire house has been thoroughly examined. Cadaver dogs from South Wales Police will also play a key part in the examination of the property; these dogs can detect minute traces of blood or human remains even if it has been there for many years. We are also receiving assistance from colleagues from other agencies who are providing specialist search equipment.'

He confirmed that the police appeal over the Volvo S80, which Halliwell had once owned, had produced a number of leads. Memory thought he had found the man who had bought it.

The following day the search continued and the forensics team was expanded.

'Activity at the house in Ashbury Avenue continues today with over forty staff members working on the investigation,' said Memory. 'Yesterday, blood dogs from South Wales Police scoured the property and forensically trained crime-scene investigators commenced a finger-tip search. We can confirm that a number of items of interest were found at the house and have been sent for analysis by experts.'

As well as the search, house-to-house inquiries, a poster campaign and a leaflet drop were taking place, and Memory urged anyone who saw Becky Godden over Christmas 2002 and into the New Year to get in touch.

'Detectives have been speaking to residents in the area and

gathering information regarding Becky's disappearance, this work will also continue throughout today along with the poster campaign. People have come forward with helpful information who have not contacted us previously as they didn't think it would be relevant. I cannot stress strongly enough how important it is to let us know any information you have, as the smallest detail may be the key to justice for Becky and her family. We know that Becky was last seen on December 27, 2002 and we need people to come forward with any information about where she was in early 2003. Did you see Becky over the New Year period?

'I would like to reiterate our thanks to the occupants of the house, who have no involvement in this investigation, and the local community for their assistance and co-operation. I anticipate that the road closure at Ashbury Avenue will remain in place until the end of the week.'

After five days of intensive searching, Detective Chief Inspector Memory announced: 'Work is now complete at the house and a number of items have been sent for forensic analysis. The results of these tests are expected to take some weeks. The investigation continues and further lines of inquiry have been developed following the new witnesses who came forward as a result of the activity this week.

'We are extremely grateful to everyone who has assisted us, the residents in Ashbury Avenue have been very supportive and we hope that the disruption has not caused too much inconvenience. This week has been very stressful for the occupants of the house, who have no involvement in the investigation, and we are very appreciative for their co-operation. We will continue to work closely with Becky's family and keep them updated with our progress.'

The renewed appeal for information seemed to have borne fruit, too.

'I am pleased with the response from the public to our latest appeal but I would still urge anyone who has information about Becky's disappearance to come forward,' said Memory. 'There will be people out there who saw her over the Christmas 2002 and New Year 2003 period and these people may hold vital details which could help us with this investigation. I can assure callers that information will be taken in the strictest confidence.'

Four days after the search of the house was complete, the disappearance of prostitute Sally Ann John in Swindon almost twenty years earlier was reopened as a murder hunt. The police said they had 'significant new lines of inquiry' and relaunched an appeal for information.

Sally Ann had been working as a prostitute in Swindon's notorious Manchester Road red light district in 1995 when she disappeared on a Friday night in early September. Some seven years later, Becky Godden, who worked in the same area, went missing. But officers played down any link between the two cases.

'At the moment the investigations are not linked and we are not treating them as linked murder inquiries,' said Detective Inspector Tim Corner, who had reclassified Sally Ann's missing-person inquiry as a murder investigation. 'It would be inappropriate for me to comment on another murder investigation, Operation Mayan, which is ongoing, but certainly at this stage they are not connected. We have a very open mind, as you do with anything we investigate.'

Asked whether he intended to speak to Halliwell, Corner replied: 'No, not at this stage, but as I say, we keep an open mind but there are no plans in relation to this investigation to speak with him or anyone else connected with Operation Mayan.'

• • •

On 14 January 2015, Karen Edwards wept as she handed her petition for changes to be made to the Police and Criminal Evidence Act into Number Ten Downing Street. It carried 42,000 signatures. She then called for police officers and patrol cars to be fitted with cameras and microphones, and insisted that the PACE rules were changed so that off-the-cuff confessions, such as the one Halliwell had given over the murder of Becky, could be used in evidence in future.

Speaking outside Number Ten, she said: 'I'm hoping the Prime Minister will look at what's happened because this isn't an isolated case. I'm hoping they'll balance our justice system out. It makes me feel very angry. It makes me feel our justice system is unjust.'

She also spoke of her own personal anguish.

'We've been on a dreadful journey,' she said. 'I've put my energy into trying to change our law, our justice system, so that other parents won't go through what we've been through. I still feel my daughter's life has been taken in vain and nobody has been convicted for her murder. That makes me feel sad.'

Others felt the same.

'I have spoken to so many people who have had a similar experience to me,' she added. 'They have had an injustice. If we had something that would back up everything, it is there in black and white, you cannot argue with that. The law has a lot of grey areas and this is one of them.'

The presence of cameras would also help protect innocent people against potential mistreatment and miscarriages of justice.

'It protects both sides,' she said. 'That is why PACE was put there in the first place. So why not protect them even more by adding cameras?'

A spokeswoman for the Home Office said: 'The Police and Criminal Evidence Act and its codes of practice are designed to protect the rights of all those in the criminal justice system, including victims and interviewing officers. The act was introduced as a direct response to concerns over the conduct of the police in significant miscarriages of justice in the early 1980s and has stood the test of time ever since.

'The codes are regularly reviewed in consultation with the police and other stakeholders, and updated where this is considered to be necessary. We are committed to ensuring that the police can maximise the use of new technologies, including body-worn video, for the purposes of reducing crime and dealing with offenders.'

CHAPTER SEVENTEEN

BROUGHT TO BOOK

Finally, the Wiltshire Police's persistence paid off. The new evidence uncovered included forensic analysis of soil from a spade and garden tools found in Halliwell's shed and fresh witness statements. One witness saw Miss Godden getting into a taxi in early January 2003 – this was just days after the last confirmed sighting of her by a police officer in Swindon in December 2002. Another witness saw Halliwell and a woman, whom he believed to be Becky Godden, arguing in a pub in Eastleach at that time.

On 30 March 2016, Halliwell was charge with the murder of Becky Godden some time between 1 January 2003 and 3 April 2008. The following day, he appeared before magistrates in Chippenham. The case was referred to Bristol Crown Court, where Halliwell appeared by video link on 1 April.

The taxi driver was wearing a brown jacket and white

T-shirt. He was accused of killing Rebecca Godden between 2003 and 2008. He did not enter a plea and spoke only to confirm his name. Karen Edwards and the family looked on from the public gallery.

Appearing again via video link from Long Lartin on 9 June, Halliwell denied murdering Becky. Wearing a brown T-shirt and glasses, he then announced that he had fired his legal team and would represent himself.

Mr Justice Openshaw told the court: 'If he needs access to law books, everything should be done to ensure that he can properly prepare for his defence.'

Steps would also be taken to ensure Halliwell could have his papers and a table in the dock, from where he would cross-examine witnesses.

Again, Becky's mother Karen Edwards, stepfather Charlie Edwards, and father John Godden, sat in the packed public gallery of courtroom two. Prosecutor Nicholas Haggan QC said a hundred witnesses, including nine experts, could give evidence during the trial. A further pre-trial hearing would take place in July.

The judge remanded Halliwell into custody and told him: 'OK, Mr Halliwell, I will now speak to the trial judge to suggest that he arranges a date towards the end of July and the case will be mentioned again for a series of further orders to be made.'

The trial judge was to be retired High Court judge Sir John Griffith Williams. Mr Justice Openshaw had also made arrangements with the prosecution.

'I have suggested to Mr Haggan that he produce a document setting out the hundred or so witnesses who presently are to give evidence against you, and setting out very briefly the nature of the evidence they are to give, and you should indicate whether you require them to attend in person,' he said.

After two days of legal arguments at a preliminary hearing in July, Justice Griffith Williams ruled that Halliwell's confession could now be presented to the jury. The judge also stated that the jury could be told of Halliwell's conviction for murdering Sian O'Callaghan, as well as admissions the taxi driver made to a police doctor. Following his arrest, Halliwell told Dr Nazir Ali that he was being detained at Gablecross Police Station in Swindon because he had 'killed two people'.

Police believed Halliwell abducted Miss Godden in early 2003 from the Destiny & Desire nightclub, close to where he took Sian O'Callaghan.

'Both were taken in a taxi,' prosecutor Nicholas Haggan QC told the hearing. 'Both bodies were deposited in rural locations on the eastern side of Swindon. Becky is believed to have been buried naked. When Sian was found she was only partially clothed.'

Halliwell appeared again on 30 August to plead not guilty to the murder of Becky Godden. Again, he confirmed that he was going to represent himself.

Speaking ahead of the trial, Karen Edwards said: 'We have been waiting for such a long time that we can't actually believe that we would get to this point. We doubted that we would get here all the time. I still feel I haven't grieved yet because I have been running on adrenaline. This is never going to bring her back. It is never going to make anything right. It is not going to bring my little girl back to me. But at the end of the day, to see him standing there… I couldn't protect Becky from him but I can do the next best thing and get justice for her. I have longed for the day. To see Halliwell have his justice. It has been my sole ambition and goal in life. Nothing else really matters.'

Halliwell, she said, made her flesh crawl.

'To think a human being could do what he did to another human being is beyond me. It really is beyond me,' she said. 'You see a child being shouted at in a supermarket and you feel like going over and saying, "Do you know how precious that child is?"'

Karen said Becky was 'a very intelligent little girl at school'.

'She always liked to be top of the class and she used to like reading – she was a right bookworm,' she added. 'She loved animals, she absolutely adored animals. Like any little girl, she wanted to be a princess.'

She was also a beautiful child as well as a little devil when drugs took hold of her in her teens.

'There were lots of twists and turns to Becky's life and it took her down a very dark road,' Karen said. 'I had to wake up and smell the roses very quickly. I learned a side of life that I knew nothing about before. I just did what any mother would do.'

She added: 'It was a real struggle but I never in a million years thought this was what was going to happen. All of her life was two steps forward and three steps back. And I still feel like it is like that now. There were always twists and turns. She never chose for this to happen.'

The trial began at Bristol Crown Court on 5 September. Halliwell appeared wearing a grey suit, a crisp white shirt and a light-blue tie. Now bald, he carried a large bundle of documents with him into the dock, where he was protected by a glass screen. Becky's family were in the courtroom, along with Sian's mother Elaine and her boyfriend Kevin.

'I didn't want to sit at home and read about it,' Elaine told *The Sun*. 'I knew they were going to use Sian's case as evidence, and if anything was going to be said about her, I wanted to be there.'

She knew it would be an ordeal, as four-and-a-half years earlier she had sat through Halliwell's trial for the murder of her daughter.

'I'd never really heard him speak before,' said Elaine. 'But he took the stand and described in graphic detail how Sian was killed. As he pleaded guilty to her murder, this was the first time it was said in open court, so in a way it was harder than before.

'Over the next few days it felt like I was living in two different worlds. There was my regular life, dropping Aiden at school in the morning, and then an hour later sitting in court with Sian's murderer. It was very intense and at the end of each day I would have a massive headache.'

No matter how painful it was, she stuck to her guns.

'Every day I made sure I sat in the seat closest to him – sometimes no more than a foot away,' Elaine said. 'I wasn't going to let him intimidate me. We made eye contact a few times, but he always ended up looking away.'

As there was now corroborating forensic evidence, Halliwell's confession in March 2011 became key to the prosecution. Nicholas Haggan QC told a jury of six men and six women: 'Christopher Halliwell confessed to the police that between 2003 and 2005 – he couldn't be sure of the date – he had taken a girl from the streets of Swindon. He told the police he had sex with her and then he killed her by strangling her. He told the police he stripped the girl of her clothes and concealed her naked body. Not only that, but the defendant took the police to the location.'

As the evidence of his confession was given, Halliwell looked distracted and twirled his reading glass, or glared at the victims' families and the press in the public gallery.

Mr Haggan went on: 'Had the defendant not told the police where he had buried that girl from the streets of Swindon, you might think that Rebecca's remains to this day would be in that field in the middle of nowhere.'

The jury was also told that Halliwell had admitted murdering Sian O'Callaghan, who had disappeared outside the Suju nightclub in Swindon in March 2011. Her semi-naked body was discovered in undergrowth in Uffington, shortly after Halliwell was arrested in connection with her kidnapping.

The jury were told that it was at this point that Halliwell told Detective Superintendent Fulcher, who was leading the investigation for Wiltshire Police: 'We need to have a chat. I am a sick f*****. Is it too late to get help?'

He then asked the detective if he wanted 'another one'. Fulcher was eager to discover where the victim had been buried.

'The superintendent asked, "Would you be able to take us to the vicinity?" and the defendant replied, "Exact spot",' Mr Haggan said. 'Mr Fulcher asked whether there were any others and the defendant replied, "No, isn't that enough?"'

On the way to the place the second victim was buried, Halliwell had said to Fulcher: 'I know you are not a psychiatrist, but what the f***'s wrong? Normal people don't go round killing each other.'

The court heard that, in return for a cigarette, Halliwell then directed officers to Oxo Bottom field in Eastleach, where the skeletal remains of Becky Godden – later identified by DNA – were discovered.

Traces of soil found on a shovel in Halliwell's garden shed match samples taken from Becky's grave, the court heard. The jury was told that the soil taken from the boundary of Oxo Bottom field where Becky was buried was 'virtually unique'. Experts believed that the soil's characteristics, including its colour and texture, meant the chance of that combination being replicated was negligible. A roll of black tape, with traces of the same soil on it, was also found at Halliwell's home.

After he was arrested, the jury were told, he told the station doctor Nazir Ali, who was called in to assess his mental state: 'I have killed two people.'

Halliwell had pleaded guilty to murdering Sian O'Callaghan and was jailed for life in October 2012. Mr Haggan then claimed that there was 'no doubt of any sort' that Halliwell was also responsible for then murder of Becky Godden.

'Her naked body was buried in a clandestine grave in a field which might be described as in the middle of nowhere,' Mr Haggan said. 'You might conclude that it was plain Rebecca was murdered. But secondly, this defendant, Christopher Halliwell, confessed… The defendant says he didn't murder Rebecca Godden. We say it cannot be clearer that he did. There isn't a shred of doubt, not even a sliver.'

The court was told that Becky had started using Class A drugs and became a prostitute in her mid-teens, working in the Manchester Road area of Swindon. Despite her lifestyle, Becky kept in contact with her family, especially on Mother's Day and her birthday. But Karen Edwards had seen her daughter for the last time on 16 December 2002, when she collected her from Swindon Magistrates' Court and drove her to a friend's house in the town.

A community beat officer recorded seeing her on 27 December 2002 and Becky's friend Rebecca Boast told police she saw her get into a taxi outside the Swindon nightclub Destiny & Desire in early January 2003, after arguing with the driver.

A taxi had pulled up and Becky went over to it. After a row, Becky returned to her companions.

'A short time later, Becky told her friends that she was leaving and she went back to the taxi,' Mr Haggan told the jury. 'She got into the rear of the vehicle and the vehicle drove away. Rebecca Boast never saw her friend again, although she looked for Rebecca when she was out and about in Swindon town centre. Extensive inquiries by the police indicate that this probably was the last known reliable sighting of Becky.'

This was in Swindon town centre in January 2003, possibly 3 January.

'After that nothing more was heard from her,' continued Mr Haggan. 'She made no contact with her family. She made no contact with any of the government and other agencies and financial institutions.'

The court heard that Miss Godden did not make contact with her family on Mother's Day in 2003, nor on her twenty-first birthday in April that year.

'She quite literally disappeared,' Mr Haggan said. 'She was just twenty years old.'

Justice Griffith Williams, warned the jurors they should not assume that Halliwell's conviction for murdering Miss O'Callaghan made him guilty of killing Miss Godden.

'The prosecution case against Mr Halliwell, which will be developed this afternoon, is that there are similarities between the circumstances of the killing of Sian O'Callaghan and the killing of Becky Godden,' the judge said. 'The prosecution case is that these similarities are such that they prove the defendant was the killer of Rebecca or Becky Godden. That is one of the issues in the case and you will have to decide, on the evidence as you hear it, whether there are such similarities and whether that inference can be drawn from those similarities. What you must not do is assume or conclude from the fact that he has pleaded guilty to the murder of Sian O'Callaghan. That would be wholly wrong.'

The prosecution introduced evidence that would put Halliwell on the spot. At 5.25 a.m. on that morning, Mr Haggan said Halliwell logged a call with the RAC reporting that his Volvo S80 had run out of fuel on the A361 at Inglesham, near Lechlade-on-Thames, less than five miles from Eastleach.

'In the early hours of the morning on 3 January he had driven to a spot not a million miles away from Eastleach,' the prosecutor said. 'You might want to ask yourself what Mr Halliwell was doing on the A361 at Inglesham in the early hours of the morning of 3 January 2003.'

That afternoon, Halliwell went to his GP, Dr Philip Mayes, complaining of a swollen right hand, and was diagnosed with a suspected fractured finger. In his notes, Dr Mayes recorded that Halliwell had multiple scratches to his face and appeared 'emotionally distressed'. Halliwell had told the doctor he was assaulted by a man who grew annoyed when he refused to pick him up from the street in his taxi. But Halliwell's employment diary did not show him working between 1 January and 4 January, although this was not reported to police.

As the trial continued, the jury heard that Christopher

Halliwell was seen pouring a drink over Becky Godden and abusing her verbally shortly before she was murdered.

Trevor Puffitt knew of Becky Godden after being propositioned by her on the Magic Roundabout in Swindon in about 2000, the jury heard. Three years later, he was in Eastleach to visit his parents' graves and went to the Victoria Inn. Puffitt said he was sitting in the beer garden when he overheard a couple arguing.

'The male was very aggressive towards the girl,' Mr Haggan said. 'He shouted at her. He told her she was a 'f★★★ing slag'. He threw a drink over her and pushed her about.'

Puffitt stood up and challenged the man, who walked off. He then approached the woman.

'It was at that point he realised that the girl he was speaking to was the same girl who had propositioned him on the Magic Roundabout some three years or so earlier,' Mr Haggan said.

Things fell into place later.

'Time moved on and in 2011 Mr Puffitt became aware of the murder of Sian O'Callaghan,' said Mr Haggan. 'He saw images of the defendant and Sian in a local newspaper. He also saw an image of Becky in the newspaper. He then recognised the defendant and Becky as the couple who had been arguing in the Victoria Inn.'

The court also heard that Kevin Yule, a friend of Halliwell, had recommended the Victoria Inn in Eastleach to him.

In police interviews in February 2015, Halliwell appeared to offer a deal in which he would admit Becky's murder if police then left him alone. Later, he told his daughter Natasha Halliwell: 'I got it off my chest. I've offered them, as far as I'm concerned, the goose that lays the golden egg. And they've let it fly away.'

A Swindon prostitute, referred to in court as Miss X, then gave evidence. She said that Halliwell was a regular client of Becky's. She knew him as 'Chris' and would often see his car parked near the red light district in Swindon where she and Becky worked. They even discussed the relationship she had with him.

'I would say "Does he take you to score?" and she would say no, he was just one of her regulars,' Miss X told the court. 'She did not go into much detail in the conversation on that occasion. We had another one and she was just like sometimes he does her head in.'

Was he obsessed with her?

'I'm not a hundred per cent sure, but he was always parked there,' said Miss X. 'That might have put the person off who's parking up to a girl. Nothing that rang alarm bells to me. He was always wanting her to go with him and stuff. He was just a bit besotted. To be honest, I think Becky used to use him for a lift to score and stuff, but I think he might have seen it as a bit more than that and I think it might have done her head in. At first he would give her money to stop her from working.'

She suspected that Halliwell took Becky to Bristol to buy drugs in exchange for sex.

Miss X also claimed that Halliwell had been her customer on two occasions.

'I would obviously recognise him because I've been up close and personal with him,' she told the jury.

On the first occasion, they had sex on an industrial estate in Swindon, and on another they went to a flat. On the second occasion, Halliwell showed Miss X images of 'Thai brides' on his desktop computer, she said. Later, Halliwell gave Becky and Miss X a lift to buy drugs.

'He said, "Don't mention to Becks that I have seen you,"' Miss X told the court. She also claimed that during a conversation with Halliwell, he told her he could not always afford to give Becky money.

During cross-examination, Halliwell insisted Miss X was mistaken. He claimed he had never spoken to Miss X before.

'I don't have to tell you how serious this matter is,' he told her from the dock. 'Please take a good, hard look at me and confirm the person you are thinking of is me.'

Miss X stared at Halliwell and replied flatly: 'It definitely is you.'

Halliwell later told the jury: 'I've never seen that woman before… it is a fairytale.'

But Miss X was insistent.

'I don't understand how he can sit there and say he doesn't know me,' she said. 'I'm a hundred, million per cent sure.'

Halliwell drew gasps from the public gallery when he asked her what colour his eyes were.

'What colour were Becky's eyes?' she replied tartly.

Miss X's story was confirmed by another Swindon sex worker, Miss Y. Still Halliwell was insistent.

'I never knew Rebecca,' Halliwell told the jury. 'I certainly didn't take her for a drink.'

The court was told that Halliwell was a regular user of prostitutes.

'After Lisa had Shane in 1996 she went completely off sex, I didn't,' he had told the police. 'I'm not going to say I was out there every single night trying to get it. I wanted to get it out of my system, I didn't want an affair, I didn't want a relationship. Occasionally, I would use a call girl. They work in a certain area around Swindon. There's no emotional involvement. Obviously, with an affair there's a danger you get too emotionally involved and it would ruin your marriage. It was a sensible escape rather then getting into an affair.'

Steve Fulcher, by then a security consultant in Somalia, was called by the prosecution to give evidence about what Halliwell had told him on the day of his arrest on suspicion of kidnapping Sian O'Callaghan in March 2011.

The jury heard how Halliwell had been arrested in an Asda car park in Swindon and driven to the Uffington area with Fulcher, police civilian Deborah Peach and Detective Sergeant Edward Strange. At the location where Miss O'Callaghan's body was later found, Fulcher said Halliwell told him 'We need to have a chat.'

As Yvonne, his wife of twenty-eight years, looked on from the public gallery, Fulcher confirmed he asked Halliwell what he wanted to say.

'He replied "I am a sick f*****" and he asked if it was too late to get help,' Fulcher told the court. 'I replied, "It's gone beyond that, Chris."'

The court heard there was a pause and then Halliwell said: 'Another one.'

Fulcher said: 'He could not be clear about the year and that he had taken a prostitute from the Manchester Road area of Swindon. I asked if he was able to take us back to the vicinity and he replied, "Exact spot." He said, "I know you're not a psychiatrist but what the f***'s wrong? Normal people don't go round killing each other."'

Fulcher was keen to know if there were any more victims. 'I asked if there were any more incidents,' he told the court. "Did you do one in February?" He said no. I asked only those two and he replied, "Isn't that enough?" I said, "Yes it is" and asked him "When we find Sian are we going to find anything disturbing – was it straight sex?" He replied, "Didn't have sex."'

According to Fulcher, Halliwell also asked him: 'What caught me?'

The detective told the court: 'I said, "We have been surveilling you."

'He said, "At Heathrow last night?"

'I said, "Yes," and he replied, "I might be sick but I'm not f***ing stupid."

'Later in the conversation he said, "I can't explain it to myself. I don't think I will be getting community service."

'I replied, "No, you won't."'

He later told the police officer that he had picked a prostitute up and had sex with her before strangling her to death, the court heard.

Halliwell then directed Detective Sergeant Strange to a ploughed field at Eastleach where he said he had buried the other body. Locating a dip in a wall around the edge of Oxo Bottom field, Halliwell paced out to the spot where he said he had buried the body, the court heard.

Fulcher continued: 'Halliwell told me had had left the body at the edge of the field and that he had returned the following night, spent all night digging a five-foot grave to bury the body. He told me he had last visited the site about three years ago.'

Becky's body was later discovered exactly the same distance away from the wall, but from a different dip that was covered in vegetation, the court heard. After that, Halliwell was arrested, put in an unmarked police car and taken to Gablecross Police Station in Swindon.

Cross-examining the former police officer, Halliwell challenged Fulcher on how deep Becky's body had been buried. Fulcher said that Halliwell had told him that he had buried his victim in a grave five-foot deep, but the body was found in a grave that was just six to eight inches deep.

'You know from your inquiries that I spent most of my working life as a ground worker or building,' Halliwell told him. 'So in that capacity I knew the difference between a five-foot hole and a six-inch hole. Doesn't it stand out?'

'It does stand out,' said Fulcher. 'What I inferred from that, Christopher, is that Becky is one of your victims, as is Sian and you got confused about the nature of this deposition. You described very clearly a five-foot hole. You couldn't remember whether it was three or four or five. That led me to conclude that there are other victims.'

Halliwell suggested another possibility.

'Doesn't that suggest that maybe I didn't know?' he said. 'By the end of this process you will know the truth about my involvement. It is going to leave a hell of a lot of questions unanswered. I was a ground worker. If I had dug a hole, I would have known how deep it was. The first time I was in that field was with you.'

He concluded: 'By the way, it was a pleasure ruining your career. You corrupt bastard.'

The following day, the jury heard that when it was excavated by police in 2011, Becky's skeleton was missing bones including her skull and arms. Forensic archaeologist Professor John Hunter told the court that the grave was between thirty-five and forty centimetres deep.

'I identified four possibilities to explain the absence of the upper arms and head,' he said. 'There were no trauma marks to suggest that the head and arms had been removed before burial. In terms of scavenging by animals, it is unusual that the degree of scavenging should be selective to just the head and arms. The third possibility was that the head and arms had been removed by ploughing. I would have expected to find missing components within the immediate vicinity given the way the field had been ploughed. There was no evidence of that. Finally, that the body was revisited and the head and arms removed. This would explain why some of the parts of the anatomy were out of anatomical position.'

The jury heard that some of Becky's teeth were found in her chest cavity.

In a statement read to the court, consultant forensic anthropologist Dr Nicholas Marquez-Grant said between fifty per cent and seventy-five per cent of Miss Godden's skeleton had been recovered. Dr Ashley Fegan-Earl, a consultant pathologist, said he could not ascertain a cause of death. However, he had determined that all the bones in the grave belonged to Miss Godden.

The jury heard that soil samples were taken from Oxo Bottom field, tape found in the grave there, and a spade with black tape attached to it found in Halliwell's shed following his arrest in March 2011. Professor Lorna Dawson, a forensic soil scientist, said it was likely the soil samples from the spade and tape had come from the field.

'The chance of finding such similarities of soils from other samples from elsewhere is negligible,' Professor Dawson told the court. 'You can never say never because there might be somewhere else, but we never saw it in over five hundred samples that we compared it with. There's nothing as seen with the samples we found on the silver tape, the black tape and the spade and Oxo Bottom field.

'All the soil on the silver tape – one-hundred per cent – is likely to have come from Oxo Bottom field. About fifty per cent of the soil that came from the black tape is likely to have come from the field. About sixty per cent of the soil that came from the spade is likely to have come from Oxo Bottom field.'

The court was told the texture, colour, alkanes, alcohol content, organic matter and mineralogy of the soils had all been compared by experts. Professor Dawson described the soil from Oxo Bottom field as 'sticky' and said it would 'adhere to something that it came into contact with'.

Cross-examining the expert witness from the dock, Halliwell asked her whether the spades found in his shed would be able to dig a grave in the field.

'I didn't measure the penetration resistance of the soil in that field, so I cannot comment on the particular strength of the tools,' she replied.

'I can assure you that they are not,' Halliwell told the court. 'I have worked on over two hundred properties in that area. Those shovels aren't capable of going anywhere close to getting through that field. I've seen thirty-six-tonne excavators break their teeth trying to get through that limestone.'

The jury heard that Halliwell had undergone three interviews at Worcester Police Station and appeared to offer police a deal to resolve the case. He told officers: 'If I get charged with this and found guilty, I'll get a natural [a whole-life order]. That's it. Curtains, over. I mean, I'm not being funny. I'm fifty now, but twenty-five years to go, so chances are not looking good as it is. If I wrap this up in the next few hours, any other charges against me that will be brought, that's bits of past. I think you probably know about various things in the past, there's car thefts, break-ins, bits and pieces, some more serious. Will that… will clearing this up be enough to stop everything else? If I can clear this up in the next few hours, will everything else be forgotten?'

It seemed he wanted to be left in peace.

'I can resolve the matter but I don't want you coming back every couple of years, every five years, every ten years, whatever, with this,' he said. 'I'm sick of it. If it goes to court and I'm found guilty, that's it, they're locking me up and throwing away the key. I'm under no illusion, I'm not stupid so be that it.'

During the interviews, which were filmed, Halliwell had been given a letter by Detective Superintendent Memory stating that he was not aware of any other ongoing investigations. Halliwell asked for the letter to be rewritten, adding: 'There aren't any outstanding crimes that are as serious as murder, without doubt.'

He later was asked a series of thirty-one questions about Becky's case and replied 'no comment' to each one. The court was also told that Halliwell had called his daughter Natasha from prison at 10.23 a.m. on 22 February and spoke to her about the interviews.

'On Wednesday I was taken out of here and rearrested for Becky,' Halliwell said in the phone call, which was recorded. 'I spoke to Detective Superintendent Sean Memory, the bloke in charge of the case. I said, "I will help you if I can but I want something in return." They gave me a bit of paper that was way, way, way short of what I asked for, but I have it in writing that the police don't want me for anything else.

I got it off my chest. As far as I am concerned, I have offered them the goose that lays the golden egg and they have let it fly away. I'm not going to say anything without any safeguard for you lot.'

Conducting his own defence, Halliwell forced his former partner Heather Widdowson to come to court and face him. She was so terrified of him that she was allowed to give evidence from behind a screen. Trembling as she addressed the jury, she shook so much that she could barely lift a plastic cup to her lips to take a sip of water.

In the event, Halliwell declined to ask her any questions. This drew a rebuke from the judge, but Halliwell said he did not ask her any questions because she was so upset.

CHAPTER EIGHTEEN

'NO REASON
TO LIE'

Taking the witness box in his own defence, Halliwell told the court: 'I want to start by saying I am telling the truth. I have no reason to lie – getting life anyway and I have no real prospect of getting out and I deserve every day anyway. What happened between me and Sian – my actions were brutal. What I put Sian's family through was inhuman. Whether I get out or not is irrelevant; whether you the jury find me guilty or not guilty, doesn't matter. I come here to tell the truth.'

Dressed in a short open-necked striped blue-and-white shirt, he came up with a fantastic story. Over a period of three years starting in 2001, he said he would regularly drive two men around various addresses in Swindon late at night. He thought they were drug dealers.

'I never asked any questions – I didn't want to know,' he said. 'I am a taxi driver and I was turning a blind eye. That's their business. It may be morally wrong but it wasn't my place to judge someone.

'After the second or third occasion – it went on for years – taking them around various addresses in Swindon and dropping them off at the station, they commented: "You never ask any questions."

'I said: "It is none of my business and if we get stopped it is not my problem. I have no interest in what you are doing." If they are going to pay me three or four times more than the taxi fare – that's paying my bills, paying my mortgage for my family. I'd rather they were paying me than another driver.'

Halliwell told the court that in March 2003 he received a phone call from the men.

'They said something has gone wrong and they needed to get rid of something,' he said. 'I was a taxi driver and knew the area outside of Swindon and they asked did I know of anywhere they could get rid of something for a while. I was under the impression it was temporary and they said as much and in a few weeks they would recover whatever they would get rid of and hiding. I took them to Eastleach.

'When I picked them up, one of them opened the boot and they put a large sports bag in the boot. I didn't ask any questions. I assumed it was either drugs, money, possibly weapons.'

Flanked by police officers and security guards, Halliwell gripped the sides of the witness box as he gave evidence. He was just a few metres away from Sian and Becky's grieving families, seated in the packed public gallery. The defendant paused to compose himself every so often and sucked on a blue asthma inhaler.

He went on to tell the jury that he left the two men in

the field. When he returned an hour later, he could see in the car's headlights that the two men were standing in the location he later identified to the police.

'I didn't know at the time they had buried Rebecca. I was under the impression it was drugs, money or weapons, I didn't know, I didn't ask,' Halliwell insisted. 'The fact is they said it was temporary. They gave the indication that the reason they were getting rid of what they were getting rid of was that things were coming on top for them and for a while they had to hide whatever they were dealing in.'

After he dropped the two men back in Swindon, they gave him £600 or £700 in cash. On the last occasion he had any dealing with the men, there was just one of them. He sat in the front passenger seat high on drugs.

'I never made inquiries with him about what happened at Oxo Bottom field, but he volunteered the information that when they went out there they had buried a prostitute from Swindon,' he said. 'I thought he was messing about. It was right up to March 26 or 27, 2011. I always wondered if he was bullshitting because I never asked any questions. I thought he was messing about. He said it like it was nothing. It didn't seem to bother him.'

Halliwell said he was unsure whether the man – whom he repeatedly refused to name in court – was telling the truth and he did not speak to him again.

After leading Detective Superintendent Fulcher to Sian's body in Uffington, Halliwell told the jury he had volunteered: 'Do you want to go for another one?' He had then directed police to the field where Becky's remains were buried. Fulcher repeatedly refused Halliwell's requests for a solicitor and to be taken to a police station. Halliwell claimed Fulcher had threatened one of his children while they were at Barbury Castle, when he was asking where Sian O'Callaghan was, and he wanted to exact revenge.

'It was important to recover Sian,' Halliwell told the jury. 'I then bought time to keep myself out of the police station, not so much for my benefit, as I had asked several times for a solicitor. I used that refusal by Mr Fulcher to look for revenge for threatening my children. In reality, I couldn't care less about not being cautioned, refused a solicitor, threats of the press.'

He then led Fulcher to Oxo Bottom field where he believed two drug dealers had buried a prostitute in 2003, he said.

'I was unaware if there was a body in that field of Oxo field,' he claimed. 'If there was, she would be recovered. I didn't know about PACE. I didn't know about these codes, but I knew enough that if I asked to speak to a solicitor everything should stop before that has been afforded. I knew that much. I knew what was going on wasn't right.'

The court previously heard evidence that while driving to Eastleach, Halliwell told Detective Superintendent Fulcher he had strangled a prostitute from Swindon and buried her there.

'What I said to Fulcher on the way to Eastleach was a load of lies,' Halliwell told the court. 'When Mr Fulcher threatened one of my kids I used a lack of caution, the repeated refusal of a solicitor, to my advantage. My advantage was keeping myself out of the police station for as long as I possibly could at the same time as asking for a solicitor repeatedly. The longer I stayed out of the police station the longer he [Fulcher] could be in trouble for not abiding to PACE.'

He insisted: 'None of what I did makes sense. Whether

you, the jury, find me guilty or not guilty – I couldn't care less. I have nothing else to say, thank you.'

Judge Griffith Williams asked Halliwell why he had said 'no comment' in answer to police questions in interviews after his arrest.

'Simple,' replied Halliwell. 'If I said anything to the police, Fulcher would have got away with threatening my kids. As twisted as it is, what I did to Sian, I was going to do everything I could to destroy his career, basically get revenge for what he said at Barbury Castle about my kids.'

Halliwell denied it was his taxi Rebecca Boast had seen Becky Godden getting into outside the Destiny & Desire nightclub, saying he had broken down at Inglesham after running out of fuel during a chauffeuring job. He claimed he was waiting for a driver from a rival firm to bring him a gallon of diesel.

After the recess for lunch, prosecutor Nicholas Haggan QC began cross-examining Halliwell and repeatedly asked him to identify the two drug dealers he claimed had buried Becky Godden. Halliwell said he knew their names but feared for his family's safety if he revealed them.

'I would sooner stay in prison and there be no repercussions for the people I care about,' he said. He was not concerned about his own safety, he said.

'Nothing is going to happen to me, you are probably right,' said Halliwell. 'I'm safely tucked up in a high-security prison, but suppose they or their associates decide to take things a bit further because they can't get hold of me? I'm safe in prison – suppose they decide to hurt me through the people I care about?'

When Mr Haggan asked how the two men had buried

the body, Halliwell said that the sports bag was big enough for a spade to fit inside, or that the men could have used their hands.

'I used to be a ground worker,' he said. 'Two reasonably healthy [people] in an hour should be able to dig a hole five foot deep, six foot long and three foot wide.'

Mr Haggan suggested Halliwell was pleading not guilty to Becky Godden's murder because he would never be released from prison if convicted.

'What murder?' said Halliwell. 'I couldn't care less if I'm found guilty of murder. I came here to give a truthful account. Not because it matters to me. There are people who want a full and truthful account more than I do.'

Mr Haggan repeated Halliwell's own words back to him: 'You thought, "I am fifty with twenty-five years to go." Not much chance but there's still a hope that you might be released when you are an old man and that's why we have a jury in place to try this case?'

'The chances of me getting out are a bit like looking for a tealight on the moon,' Halliwell responded. 'It would be very easy to just come to court, get a well-paid QC just to give an account, I plead guilty, I go back to prison. Why would I come here and put everybody through this? Why?'

Mr Haggan put it to Halliwell that he was enjoying the court process, as he liked being the centre of attention. But Halliwell was adamant.

'This is my worst nightmare,' he insisted. 'I am normally a quiet, reserved person.'

'Are you?' said Mr Haggan. 'Normally when you are not murdering young women? That wasn't your quiet persona, was it?'

Halliwell agreed: 'No, it wasn't.'

Mr Haggan described the case against Halliwell as overwhelming – particularly the evidence of the former Swindon prostitute Miss X, who said he was besotted with Becky before she disappeared.

'Your key witness is an ex-drug addict who sold herself for sex,' sneered Halliwell. 'Hardly a reliable witness, is she?'

He also denied that he had paid Miss X for sex. He did not fancy her.

'She didn't do anything for me,' he said. 'I certainly wouldn't pay her money. Not my type.'

'What is your type?' asked Mr Haggan.

'Certainly not that thing,' said Halliwell.

'Is your type size eight or size ten, pretty young woman out and about on the streets of Swindon? About five foot one or five foot two inches?' asked Mr Haggan, who then asked Halliwell whether he ever thought about the families of Sian and Becky.

'Probably every hour of the day, yes,' replied Halliwell.

Mr Haggan then accused Halliwell of keeping his defence case secret until the last possible moment. He told the jury that Halliwell had never mentioned the drug dealers before – not in police interviews, while outlining his defence case or during the trial. This was to prevent the prosecution eliminating the men from the case.

He had provided the prosecution with no outline of his case or the legal arguments he intended to advance. His cursory defence case statement merely said: 'I have no knowledge of the manner of her death, nor any information regarding details of how she died.'

Asked why he had not given the prosecution a copy of an

A4 document he was referring to, Halliwell said: 'I believe I wrote that note at 3 a.m. and I forgot to make a copy for myself.'

Mr Haggan also accused Halliwell of misleading the judge by suggesting that a list of witnesses approved by the defendant had not been given to the court. And he had scrawled notes on an official document of agreed evidence he had been asked to sign, prompting the judge to direct that those annotations did not form part of the case.

'You didn't want the prosecution to have any inkling of what you were going to say so they wouldn't have any opportunity to be checking detail,' Mr Haggan said.

'What I have to say is for the jury members,' Halliwell countered. 'I said that I would stand here and tell the absolute truth. It has got to come from me and that's why I am defending myself, albeit badly – the truth has to come from me.'

Mr Haggan pushed the point.

'It's all a complete fabrication – the story of the drug dealers and the sports bag,' he said. 'You are sitting in your cell thinking how can I get out of this and you picked your way through the prosecution case and tried to find a way round of every piece of evidence against you – the evidence against you is overwhelming.'

Halliwell continued to insist that he had been forced into making a confession to get his own back on Detective Superintendent Fulcher.

'I was dropping him in it. With the level of detail I was giving I should have been arrested and cautioned. I knew once I got to the police station he was in trouble,' Halliwell insisted. 'It had nothing to do with being refused a solicitor or taken to the police station, because he threatened my kids. He threatened one of my daughters. Had he carried out that threat it would have had an effect on my two other kids. I was in the crap anyway because I was aware I was going to be arrested for murder and I had been arrested for kidnap and I knew that was going to change to murder. In layman's terms, I was in the shit anyway and I couldn't drop myself in the shit any deeper.'

Mr Haggan then asked Halliwell to reveal details of the threat he claims Mr Fulcher made, but he refused, telling the jury: 'I wouldn't embarrass one of my girls.'

Halliwell accepted he 'loathed' Mr Fulcher and confirmed that during his cross-examination of the former Wiltshire officer he had called him a 'corrupt bastard'. But Halliwell denied that he blamed Fulcher for the situation he now found himself in. Nevertheless, he distanced himself from the confession, telling the jury: 'It wasn't a true account, it was a lie. If I had been responsible it would have been a confession. The more I lied to him the more I could see that he wasn't seeing me as a suspect; he was seeing me as a promotion, adulation, another plastic trophy in his cabinet.'

Mr Haggan asked Halliwell why he didn't say anything to the officers once he was interviewed at the police station, instead repeatedly replying 'no comment' to their questions.

'If I had spoken then Fulcher wouldn't have faced a disciplinary, would he?' said Halliwell. 'That's what it all comes down to. What he did was very wrong. After a particular police officer threatened my daughter. At the end of the lawful urgent interview, if I had been taken to the station I would have spoken once I had a solicitor.'

Mr Haggan asked why Halliwell had put Sian O'Callaghan's

family through the ordeal of pleading not guilty to murder immediately and only admitting his guilt eighteen months later, changing this plea when the case came to trial. 'You couldn't care less about anyone but yourself,' the prosecutor said.

'I do care, I am a father myself,' Halliwell told the court. 'What I put that family through was horrendous, I said that many times. I pleaded guilty once I found out Fulcher was deeply in the mire.'

But Mr Haggan pointed out: 'He wasn't. They found he acted in good faith throughout with the intention of finding Sian. He was given a final written warning, his career wasn't ruined.'

Halliwell denied that the shovel found in his shed when he was arrested in 2011 was his. He said it was already in the shed when he moved in with Heather Widdowson in 2005.

'They are scrap, you can't use them,' he said. 'It is not a digging spade, it is a coal shovel.'

Mr Haggan was insistent. 'The shovel is yours,' he told the court. 'It came from your shed. You used that implement to dig Rebecca Godden's grave. The reason her grave was shallow is that you had the wrong implement and that the ground is very hard.'

'I was not responsible for burying Rebecca,' said Halliwell.

Mr Haggan told the defendant: 'When you were arrested for Sian's murder you knew the game was up and you decided to unburden yourself and that's what you did. You made up a cock-and-bull story to try and escape a whole-life term.'

'I don't care about a whole-life term,' Halliwell replied.

The prosecution did not automatically have the right to give a closing speech to the jury when the defendant was representing himself. But Mr Haggan pointed out: 'This is a man who goes into the witness box and is not overawed at being asked questions by Queen's Counsel suggesting that he is guilty of murder.'

The judge ruled that closing speeches could be given in the interests of fairness, describing the defendant as 'intelligent and articulate'.

'It is obvious to me that he has put his case selectively to the jury, that he has deliberately withheld details of his defence to the last minute,' Sir John Griffith Williams said.

In the closing speech for the prosecution, Mr Haggan said that it was clear Halliwell had lied time and time again in his evidence. He described the taxi driver as 'smug' and drew a comparison between the murder of Sian O'Callaghan and that of Becky Godden. Both women were young, attractive, with a slight build and had disappeared from the streets of Swindon in the early hours of the morning. Both women were strangled and their bodies were left in rural locations not very far from each other.

'The defendant did as he had confessed,' Mr Haggan told the jury. 'He took Rebecca from the streets of Swindon. He strangled her. He had sex with her. He buried her in Oxo Bottom field. He murdered her. He is guilty. All that he has told you about the drug dealers and the bag is a fairytale.'

He repeated that there was not 'a shred of doubt, not even a slither' that would mean Halliwell was not guilty.

The following day, in his closing statement from the dock, Halliwell told the jury: 'Let's look at the so-called evidence the prosecution have. Two former drug addicts who contradict themselves repeatedly in their statements. An RAC mechanic who remembers nothing. Rebecca Boast, who was such a good friend of Rebecca Godden she didn't report it for three years and nine months. She didn't see the taxi driver's face. Trevor Puffitt who stood in the witness box and said in a very vague manner that it was me.'

He was equally dismissive of the evidence concerning the soil on the shovel: 'The forensics evidence so poorly presented to the forensic lab, so poorly examined, it is not worth mentioning. It is rubbish.'

Then there was the story about him leading the police to the grave by feeling for a dip in a wall and paced to a spot in the field before telling officers: 'She's here.'

'The reference point was the concealed dip in the wall,' Halliwell told the jury. 'How could anyone take a reference from a dip in the wall that is invisible? Do I need to say more?'

Then he turned to the judge and said: 'Thank you, my lord, I am finished.'

Justice Griffith Williams then began his two-hour summing up.

'Becky's young life was unhappily characterised by drug abuse and prostitution but was no less valuable,' he said. He told the jury: 'Put out of your mind any thoughts of hostility or sympathy, whichever way they lie. All the answers you need can he found in the evidence. A judge in front of whom I appeared many years ago directed juries that if they kept their feet on the ground their heads would not be in the clouds.'

Speaking of Halliwell's conviction for the murder of Sian O'Callaghan, the judge said: 'You must bear in mind that it is a part of the evidence that may be considered along with all the other evidence in the case. Halliwell has said he did not know Miss Godden and that two drug dealers were responsible for her death. The prosecution say this is an utter fabrication and in an attempt to avoid conviction.'

He pointed out that the court had been told Halliwell initially confessed to strangling Miss Godden and led police to the exact spot where her remains were found. The court also heard that during an interview conducted on 23 February, Halliwell made references to serving a whole-life term for Becky's murder.

'He said, "If I get charged with this and found guilty, I'll get a natural, that's it, curtains, over,"' the judge repeated.

Speaking of Halliwell's defence, the judge said Halliwell had alleged he had picked up two drug dealers from Swindon railway station who admitted killing Becky.

'They said they had buried a prostitute from Swindon as if it was nothing. He said he was horrified because he had children of his own,' he continued.

The court heard Halliwell denied knowing former sex worker Miss X, who had previously alleged that Becky had a client, a taxi driver called Chris.

Justice Griffith Williams said that when Halliwell was arrested on 23 February 2015. he was asked if he had killed Becky and he replied 'no comment'.

'He said he was already up to his neck and was dropping Steve Fulcher in it, he refused to say what that was,' the judge said. 'He reported he had told lies, he reported he had wanted to make things worse for Steve Fulcher. He said he knew where Sian O'Callaghan was buried. He said it was important to recover a body if there was one. He said he wanted revenge on Steve Fulcher. The longer he kept him away from the police station, the more trouble Steve Fulcher would get into.'

The jury then retired to consider their verdict.

CHAPTER NINETEEN

SMILED AND LAUGHED

On the afternoon 19 September 2016, cheers rang out across courtroom two at Bristol Crown Court when Christopher Halliwell was found guilty of the murder of Rebecca Godden. Halliwell smiled and laughed as the forewoman read out the unanimous verdict. The jury of six men and six women took less than three hours to convict him of the charge.

Members of Sian O'Callaghan's family and the Godden family wept and hugged each other when they heard the guilty verdict. Becky's mother Karen was in tears. Father John Godden had his head in his hands, weeping. As Halliwell was led away, he paused to stare and grin at Becky's family.

'Kevin and I were upstairs in the public gallery, where Becky's family were also seated, when the verdict was read out,' Elaine told *The Sun*. 'Even though I knew there was no way the jury wouldn't find him guilty, hearing it was a huge relief. We went for dinner that night and had some drinks with the police officers who looked after the case. I can't say it gave me closure, but in a way it was shutting the door on the legal side of things.'

Ian Harris, head of the Complex Casework Unit for the Crown Prosecution Service Wessex, issued a statement, saying: 'After Christopher Halliwell had led Wiltshire Police to the body of Sian O'Callaghan, he also confessed to the murder of Rebecca Godden, who had been missing since January 2003. That was in 2011. Since then, our focus has been to get justice for Becky and her family as well. My team in the Complex Casework Unit in CPS Wessex has worked tirelessly with Wiltshire Police to build up a strong case against Christopher Halliwell and this meant that earlier this year we were able to restart the prosecution for Becky's murder.

'In the course of his defence, Christopher Halliwell dismissed his legal team and then maintained that he had not been involved in Becky's murder. This meant we could ask the court to reverse the ruling which prevented the jury from being told about his confession.

'We succeeded and this meant that we could tell the jury not only that he was serving a life sentence for Sian's murder but also that he had confessed to Becky's murder and knew where she had been buried.

'Even then, despite all the evidence, including his own confession, Mr Halliwell continued to fight the case. In the process, he has put Becky's family through untold suffering on top of the terrible pain he has caused them by murdering Becky.

'In the end, despite his every effort to evade justice, he has been convicted, and I hope that this will finally give some comfort and closure to Becky's family. Our thoughts have been very much with them, and also with Sian's family, throughout this dreadful ordeal.'

Trial judge Sir John Griffith Williams told the court he was considering either a whole-life order or a 'significant' minimum term of imprisonment for Halliwell.

The judge said: 'I have read the mitigation of Mr Latham QC, who acted for Mr Halliwell, and the sentencing remarks of Mrs Justice Cox. They merely reinforce me in the view that he is a liar whose word should be taken in some instances with a pinch of salt.

'"Where is Savernake Forest?" His mitigation to Mrs Justice Cox is that was where he had taken Sian O'Callaghan, which is completely at odds with what he told the jury. There are a number of other discrepancies which he contradicted in his evidence on oath before this jury.'

The judge said that he believed Miss Godden had been murdered by Halliwell on the night of 2 January leading to 3 January in 2003. He would, he said, reread the sentencing remarks of Mrs Justice Cox, who sentenced Halliwell at Bristol Crown Court to life imprisonment for Sian O'Callaghan's murder, adding that when sentencing Halliwell he would put himself in the position of Mrs Justice Cox and 'consider the appropriate sentence for the murder of Sian O'Callaghan but also for the murder of Rebecca Godden'.

Outside the court, Becky's mother Karen said: 'Today Christopher Halliwell has been found guilty of Becky's murder. We have waited over five years for this momentous day. It has been an extremely painful journey, but today we have received the justice that has felt like an eternity coming for our beautiful little girl Becky. We have all sat and listened to heartbreaking evidence, day after day, to enable the jury to come to their decision. We have all sat and listened hard.

'Firstly, I would like to thank from the bottom of my heart Steve Fulcher for bringing my little girl home. I will also respect him and will be indebted to him for making that moral decision as a police officer but he should have never have suffered the terrible consequences, loss of reputation and career for doing such a thing.

'A very big thank you to Sian O'Callaghan's family for their support and I am extremely sorry that they have had to live their nightmares again. My message to any family out there who have waited so long for justice as we have is never give up hope.'

Detective Superintendent Memory said that Halliwell could have had more victims but was not currently linked to any unsolved murders.

'I am really open minded there may be others – there is an eight-year gap between Becky and Sian,' he said. 'I would appeal to Christopher Halliwell, actually – if he wants to speak, I'm willing to speak with him. I can't rule out that there are other victims; however I have no direct evidence at the moment to suggest there are. What I can say is that he's not forensically linked to outstanding cases. However that's not to say he hasn't committed other offences.'

Asked if Halliwell had the potential to kill others, Memory said: 'I've no doubt. He's demonstrated at this trial his ability to lie, his ability to kill women who both in their own way were very vulnerable.'

He later pledged to redouble the investigation.

'I will now go away and look at the timeline of Christopher Halliwell,' said Memory. 'He's been a taxi driver up and down the country, he's been a ground worker up and down the country, and I'll look to other police forces to find out if they have missing people in very similar circumstances. I can't rule out that there are other victims. I'm not specifically looking at any one particular offence, but I want to try to understand why there's an eight-year gap.'

He also questioned why Halliwell had tried to strike a deal with police where he implied he would confess to Becky's killing if granted immunity from future prosecution.

Asked what he thought about the actions of Fulcher, he said he could not comment on whether the Independent Police Complaints Commission were right to find Fulcher accountable, but added: 'There is a possibility that Becky may well have remained where she is now, in an undignified clandestine grave, had he not acted. That doesn't necessarily make it right but at least we have brought closure.'

Sian's mother Elaine also said she thought Halliwell could have killed other women.

'Halliwell may have gone on to do others,' she said. 'We'll never know, will we? As far as I'm concerned, I think there would be others. I don't know when. I don't think a man started killing at the age he killed Becky, that's my own personal take, and I don't think he'd have gone the length of time between Becky and Sian without needing his fix. Sian's suffering led to ending Halliwell's freedom, making him unable to kill again.'

She added that her family harboured no 'negative feeling' towards Mr Fulcher.

'From my point of view, I feel he shouldn't have lost his career over it, for sure, but I also understand that he made decisions that caused a legal argument,' she said.

John Godden wept outside court as he paid tribute to his daughter.

'Becky was our daughter, sister, granddaughter, niece, cousin and auntie,' he said. 'Her life was taken away too early and she will always live in our memories. Our time has come to put Becky to rest and she can now be at peace. We as a family have had some very dark days and it has been difficult for us to listen to the evidence in court and thankfully we now have some closure. We would like to thank the investigating team for all they have done and would like you all to remember Becky as she was to us – our little girl.'

Becky's seventy-seven-year-old grandmother, Miranda Godden, however, was unforgiving. 'Fulcher was a top-ranking officer with years of experience,' she said. 'Why did he make that mistake? Why didn't he read him his rights? We were so angry when we found out he had done that because we didn't get justice for Lulu [she called Becky 'Lulu' because her middle name was Louise] then and there. If he had done his job we would have done.'

She said that Fulcher's mistake had had a devastating effect on her that would stay with her until the day she died. And he had never even apologised.

'If he did apologise now, I wouldn't accept it,' she said. 'He broke the law. I have lost all the trust in the police. Their mistakes have had a devastating impact on our lives. No way in this world did Becky deserve this. Nobody deserves this.'

Furthermore, Mrs Godden called for an investigation into Wiltshire Police's handling of the case: 'They haven't learned from their mistakes and they will never learn from them… I would hate for anybody else to go through this. I wouldn't wish it on anybody. I hope it won't happen again but I know it will.'

She added: 'It has been a very long fight for justice. These last five years have been terrible. I can't talk about it without being sad, but all the tears don't bring her back. I wish they could. I would give anything. I will take this with me to my dying day. When I go, I can't go up there and say, "We didn't get any justice for you."'

Mrs Godden said that she had thought about the loss of her granddaughter constantly and recalled the day she was told that Becky was dead: 'Me and my husband were sat in the corner of the room – he was in his chair and I was sat next to him on the settee – when they came out and told us. I said, "Could you please tell me what happened to her?" and they said, "She was strangled." It is awful. It was terrible. To think that somebody has deliberately hurt one of your grandchildren. To hurt them that bad. It is just the thought of somebody really hurting her. I don't know what she went through. There were no arms, no legs, no head. No nothing.

'Becky could be having a lovely life now. She could have had a family with children. If I saw the person who did this I would just ask them "Why? Why did you do this to such a beautiful girl that had her life in front of her?" There will never be closure. Never in my lifetime. There will never be any closure. It is all I think about 24/7. I shouldn't really have her photos here, but it is like pushing her away as though she didn't exist, when she did. I look at her and think, "God, what a life she could be having now." And that Sian as well. I feel sorry for her parents as well. They got justice, so fair play to them. They got justice. Becky will be spoken about. She won't be forgotten. She will go on in our hearts and our minds for ever and ever until I come and meet her. I will meet up with her one day.'

After the trial, Steve Fulcher issued another statement defending his actions, saying the conviction proved he had done the right thing in stopping a murderer who may have gone on to kill again.

'I am very pleased that Karen Edwards has finally seen justice done for her beautiful daughter Becky, who was brutally murdered by Christopher Halliwell,' it said. 'She has fought a very dignified battle for the past five-and-a-half years to bring Halliwell to court and she should not have had to. I hope she finds some comfort in this verdict. I thank Karen for her resilience and determination to obtain justice for her beloved daughter. Halliwell is an evil and depraved violator of women.

'I did all I could to find an abducted girl, Sian O'Callaghan, in an effort to save her life, the first duty of a police officer. I also recovered a second victim of Halliwell's murder, Becky, returning her to her loved ones after eight years of their misery. I caught a serial killer, preventing any further girls being murdered. Halliwell had to be arrested as he was about to commit suicide. As the law stands, the expectation was that I should have prioritised Halliwell's right to silence and legal protection over Sian O'Callaghan's right to life.

'I remain convinced that the action that I took in allowing Halliwell to take me to the bodies of both Sian and Becky, was the right and moral thing to do. It is perfectly clear that, had I not acted as I did, neither Sian nor Becky would ever have been found and Halliwell would be free to abduct and kill other girls. When the extraordinary facts of this case are explained it is likely to lead to a public crisis of confidence in the competence and credibility of the police service.

'Despite everything that has happened to me, I cannot regret the decisions that I took that day. Ultimately, that decision ensured the return of two beautiful young women, which bought comfort to their families and ensured that Halliwell has been duly convicted of both murders.

'Now the trial is over and I am no longer a serving police officer, I am able to put these issues into the public domain for the first time. I would like to prevent any family having to suffer the same agony that Karen Edwards has had to endure. I want to ensure that any senior investigating officer, faced with crimes in action, is able to take the right decision without suffering the repercussions I experienced whilst performing my duty.'

Speculation about further victims left Halliwell's ex-wife Lisa flabbergasted. 'I do not know if there could be any more,' she said. 'He is not the person I knew. I hope the families can move on now.'

During the trial, there was one piece of information that was not put to the jury. That was the testimony of Ernest Springer, Halliwell's cellmate on Dartmoor in the 1980s. He alleged that Halliwell had asked: 'How many women do you have to kill to be a serial killer?' and 'Have you ever thought of strangling your girlfriend during sex?'

With Halliwell now convicted of a second murder, Springer talked to *The Sun*.

He repeated his claim that Halliwell had asked him 'How many people do you need to kill before you become a serial killer?' He added: 'He just had a thing about them. He used to get this magazine called *True Detective* with stories about people getting knocked off. His favourite book was about the Moors Murders, with Myra Hindley on the front.'

Justice Griffith Williams wrote in his ruling: 'The prosecution intends to rely on the following evidence [...] bad character evidence to prove the defendant's overtly aggressive conduct towards women and his computer searches on the internet for indecent and violent material [and] the evidence of Ernest Springer, with whom the defendant shared a cell at HMP Dartmoor in 1986. He said, "The defendant was angry and aggressive towards women and talked of having sex with a girl while strangling her and asked how many women one would have to kill to be a serial killer."'

Clearly, as a taxi driver, Halliwell had plenty of opportunity to cruise the streets late at night without suspicion and pick up lone women.

'No one would think it was unusual for a woman to get into a taxi,' said Dr Adam Lynes, a lecturer in criminology at Birmingham City University and author of a forthcoming book, *The Road To Murder: Why Driving is the Occupation of Choice for Britain's Serial Killers*. He points out that other serial killers, including Yorkshire Ripper Peter Sutcliffe, also drove for a living. And as a keen fisherman, Halliwell knew where in the countryside outside Swindon it would be easy to hide more bodies. However, there remains no evidence linking Halliwell with any other crime.

CHAPTER TWENTY

LIFE MEANS LIFE

Before sentencing, moving victim impact statements by Becky's mother Karen Edwards and her father John Godden were read to the court.

'Since Becky was found, my future has become very different,' Karen said. 'Tell me, how can anyone get over such an enormous ordeal and loss? Just pictures and memories, a broken heart and a grave. That is all I have left of my beautiful daughter.'

She said that the heartbreaking news of her daughter's death – delivered on what would have been her twenty-ninth birthday – would 'haunt me for the rest of my life'.

'I will never forget the day that Steve Fulcher and three other police officers knocked on my front door, to tell me the most devastating news. News that no parent should ever hear. My world had fallen apart, shattered in seconds, and that emotion I have woken up with every day since. That feeling of total devastation, disbelief, loss, pain, the flash of sudden panic that hits me in the stomach and just repulses me. It has changed my world. The world as I knew it has been totally destroyed and will never be the same, complete, ever again.

'It is such an effort some days just to get up and function. My thoughts every day are of my little girl. The little girl that can never be replaced. What must she have gone through that night? She is dead. That sends a wave of panic and pain in my chest. The only thing I can buy her is flowers for her grave. I kneel down beside her grave still disbelieving she is there. I have only been told she is dead.'

Mr Godden added: 'Having seen and heard the evidence I feel that Halliwell should have put us out of our misery as a family long ago and I am of the opinion that he has played games with us and the investigation team.'

On 24 September 2016, Sir John Griffith Williams passed a whole-life order on double murderer Christopher Halliwell and explained, in detail, why.

You have been convicted by a jury of the murder of Rebecca Godden. Sadly her young life was troubled and blighted by her drug abuse which forced her into prostitution to fund her addiction. While she had returned to the company of friends and her life of drug taking, it remained her hope that she would one day free herself of her addiction and belatedly return to her family to live the decent life her early years had promised and of which her addiction had deprived her. When you murdered her, you deprived her of a potentially fulfilling life.

Your account of the circumstances in which she

met her death bears all the hallmarks of a contrived explanation designed to avoid conviction in the hope that the minimum term you are presently serving will not be increased. But the account which you advanced so glibly with little or no regard no the truth made no sense at all.

You told Superintendent Fulcher that you had sex with an unnamed prostitute, strangled her before undressing her, then left her body in bushes by the wall at Oxo Bottom field and returned the following night to dig the grave and bury her. I am firmly of the view that that was only partially truthful.

I have had the opportunity of observing you through-out the trial and listening to your evidence. I have no doubt that you are a self-centred and domineering individual who wants his own way. You are both calculating and devious.

Having heard the evidence, I am satisfied so as to be sure to the required criminal standard of proof of the following:

1) You knew Rebecca Godden and had known her for some time. It was not a conventional relationship. I consider it unlikely that you were besotted with her. In my judgment your behaviour towards her was controlling. You used her for sex whenever you wanted to, taking advantage of her vulnerability as a drug addict and prostitute. She had little or no time for you.

2) In the early hours of 3 January 2003, when she was standing outside the Destiny & Desire club with Rebecca Boast, you drove up in your taxi and summoned her. That could only have been because you wanted her to go

with you for sex, but she was clearly not interested. She returned to join her friend but you remained and so she went to speak to you a second time. A row developed during which she yelled at you, clear evidence that she did not want to go with you. She returned again to her friend, but you did not drive off and so it was that she went to your taxi and got into a rear seat. Rebecca Boast described her as "huffed", that is to say annoyed, and I conclude she joined you unwillingly.

3) You then drove to somewhere private, most probably to the south of Swindon and to Savernake Forest, where eight years later you took Sian O'Callaghan. What then happened must be a matter of inference. I take as my starting point the evidence of your injuries when you were examined later that day by your general practitioner – a broken little finger and scratches to your face. I reject your evidence that you had been involved in a fight with a would-be passenger. I conclude you must have attacked Rebecca Godden; that attack must have been prompted by her refusing you sex. When she put up a struggle, you killed her. You clearly intended to kill her. I add that I am certain she struggled desperately in an attempt to save her life but she was physically no match for you.

4) You then drove to Oxo Bottom field, which you knew to be very isolated. There you had the presence of mind to remove her clothing to ensure, if her body was found, that there would be no forensic links to your taxi and to you. You returned the next night to bury her and returned again and again over the following years to make sure that her body was not visible in that shallow grave.

5) When on 24 March 2011 you realised you had no chance of avoiding detection for the murder of Sian O'Callaghan, you very briefly allowed the little conscience you have to prompt your confession to the murder of Rebecca Godden. I consider that but for that confession, there is every prospect that Rebecca Godden's remains would not have been found, but such mitigation that provides is overweighed in your subsequent behaviour. Following your arrest you answered 'no comment' to all questions and you have since sought to manipulate, first the police investigation and then the court process in a futile attempt to avoid the punishment you so richly deserve.

I am satisfied that your conduct amounted to abduction. Rebecca Gladden did not want to go with you and would certainly not have gone with you had she known you were prepared to rape her and to use violence if she did not do as you told her. There was clearly sexual conduct and your offending was aggravated by your concealment of the body.

As the murder was committed between 31 May 2002 and late December 2003, I must have regard to the transitional provisions in Section 276 and Schedule 22 of the Criminal Justice Act 2003 and the Practice Statement (Life Sentences) 2000 Cr App R 18, but the minimum term must reflect your culpability not only for the murder of Rebecca Godden but also for the murder of Sian O'Callaghan committed in March 2013. For that murder, the provisions of Schedule 21 of the 2003 Act apply.

Passing sentence on you for the murder of Sian O'Callaghan, Mrs Justice Cox observed that your account in mitigation bore all the hallmarks of an account clearly designed to try and explain away separate aspects of the evidence relied upon by the prosecution. She was satisfied so as to be sure that in the early hours of Saturday night, 19 March 2011, you turned your taxi handset off and then drove around the area of Swindon Old Town for some forty minutes until you saw Sian O'Callaghan.

You offered her or persuaded her to have a taxi ride home and she got into your taxi. She would have suddenly realised with horror that you were not taking her home because you drove in the opposite direction out of Swindon towards the Savernake Forest. Mrs Justice Cox rejected the suggestion that you were initially told to drive to Cottingham. In the forest, you assaulted her and murdered her and left her body somewhere in the forest area.

It was accepted you had the knife used to murder Sian O'Callaghan to use as a weapon and so the starting point was twenty-five years. Mrs Justice Cox was satisfied that you intended to kill her. At some point on Monday, 21 March, you moved her body from the place you had first hidden her to the place on the Downs where she was eventually found by the police on Thursday, 14 March 2011. Her body was partially concealed. The condition of her clothing proved that her murder involved sexual contact. There were the stab wounds to the head, deep bruising and abrasions to her face consistent with punching or kicking, and bruises and abrasions to her breasts, particularly her left breast and nipple, caused possibly by biting.

LIFE MEANS LIFE

Mrs Justice Cox said Sian O'Callaghan would have been terrified and panic-stricken right from the moment she realised you were not going to drive her home. She was satisfied that you made extensive efforts to conceal her body and would have made more but for the police activity searching the area for her. She ignored, as I shall ignore, your previous convictions, all for offences of dishonesty and committed many years ago. She allowed a discount of five years for your guilty plea and determined the minimum term as twenty-five years.

I observe that you lied to the jury about the circumstances of the murder of Sian O'Callaghan, just as you lied to the jury about the circumstances of the murder of Rebecca Godden. A feature of your evidence which I would have not been alone in considering disgracefully unfeeling was the contradiction in your claims that you wanted to spare the family of Sian O'Callaghan further grief and yet you did not take the police straight to her body, and despite your confessions to Superintendent Fulcher, you made 'no comment' answers when you were interviewed about her murder; you then pleaded not guilty and so compounded and added to the grief of her family.

You have put the family of Rebecca Godden through similar anguish, first confessing to her murder and then answering no comment to all questions in interview. After what must have been hours of trawling through the prosecution papers, you devised a cock-and-bull story about two drug dealers. I cannot add to your sentence for such cynical indifference to the concerns of the families, but it is clear to me that there is nothing which can mitigate your sentence.

I have considered the heartfelt evidence of Rebecca Godden's mother and father.

I am satisfied that there are real similarities between the two murders. The fact that some nine years elapsed between them probably reflects the absence of opportunities.

With the Transitional Provisions in mind, I have considered paragraph 18 of the Practice Statement under the heading 'Very Serious Cases' – 'A substantial upward adjustment may be appropriate in the most serious cases, for example, those involving a substantial number of murders or if there are several factors identified as attracting the higher starting point present. In suitable cases, the result might even be a minimum term of thirty years… which would offer little or no hope of the offender's eventual release. In cases of exceptional gravity, the judge, rather than setting a whole-life minimum term, can state that there is no minimum period which could properly be set in that particular case.'

I have considered also the judgment of the Court of Appeal, Criminal Division in SULLIVAN & Others [2004] EWCA Crim 1762 and in particular paragraphs 26 and 27 of the judgment.

Applying Schedule 21 of the Criminal Justice Act 2003, I have concluded both murders involved the abduction of the victim and sexual conduct, and both were aggravated by the concealment of the bodies. I am satisfied your offending is exceptionally high and satisfies the criteria for a whole-life term and that the Transitional Provisions do not require me to impose a minimum term. Were I to impose a minimum term it would be of such length that you would in all probability never be released.

I sentence you to life imprisonment and direct there will be a whole-life order.

I want in take the opportunity of saying a few words to Mrs Edwards and Mr Godden. You have had to live with every parent's nightmare of a missing child and then the discovery that she had been dead for some years, buried naked in a field. You have been deprived of the opportunity we all want, to say farewell to our closest and dearest. And then you have had to live through the criminal processes as Christopher Halliwell was brought eventually to justice. There must have been moments when you wondered whether the case would ever be completed. If I may say so, you have behaved throughout with quiet dignity and courtesy. I hope you will feel that justice has been done and that while that cannot bring Becky back, that it may at least bring you some solace.

I will include Mr and Mrs O'Callaghan because this trial must have been an ordeal for them as they had to relive the evidence of how Sian died. They too have behaved with dignity and courtesy. I pay tribute to you all.

Halliwell declined to offer any mitigation and simply said 'thank you' to the judge.

The court case was over and the families could now be certain that Halliwell would die in jail. However, that was not the end of the matter. Detectives were examining new lines of enquiry from calls that had come into their incident room. Wiltshire Police wanted to know if Halliwell had committed other offences and were working with the National Crime Agency

Speaking outside Bristol Crown Court, Karen Edwards said: 'I will never be able to give her a hug ever again and make things right for her, or take her shopping, brush her hair, have a moan at her for not keeping her room tidy or taking my make-up. No waiting up half the night for a phone call to pick her and her mates up after a night out.

'The little things we all take for granted every day. I go to the supermarket and see her favourite biscuits and sweets and I go to put them in the trolley for a split second, then I remember she is not here. She is dead. That sends a wave of panic and pain in my chest, just like a knife through my heart. The only thing I can buy her is flowers for her grave. I never had a body to kiss goodbye before she was buried.'

Becky's father, John Godden, issued a statement saying: 'The truth has been too long coming and Becky's murder has consumed me and changed me as a person and affected my trust in people. I have shut the world out and said things that I regret. Having seen and heard the evidence, I feel that Halliwell should have put us out of our misery as a family long ago and I am of the opinion that he has played games with us and the investigation team. It has killed me as a father and at times I have not been in the right place, but I do hope now that I can turn a corner and have the opportunity to move on.'

Detective Superintendent Memory made a fresh appeal for information, reminding the public that Halliwell had spoken of his desire to become a serial killer in the 1980s.

'I am also very, very clear there must be other victims out there, whether they are sexual offences or other women that he has taken,' Memory said. 'The offending behaviour for killing Becky – it was cold, it was calculating, as the judge said. I can't believe that was his first offence, from being a burglar in the 1980s to a murderer in 2003. There was a significant gap in his offending behaviour. On top of that, Sian wasn't murdered until 2011, so what happened in the interim eight years? I will now seek to review outstanding cases. I will appeal to Christopher Halliwell again to tell the truth for once in your life and come and speak to me.'

Memory was now clear on what Halliwell's methods were and now needed to take stock of what he said during the trial.

'He likes to abduct women, he likes to commit sexual offences, he likes to kill, he also likes to remove their clothing and bury them,' he said.

Memory pledged that the force would pursue Halliwell for any other offences that came to light, even though he already had a whole-life tariff and would never be allowed out.

CHAPTER TWENTY-ONE

CLEARING THE DETECTIVE'S NAME

Speaking just hours after Halliwell was sentenced to life, Karen Edwards told the *Mail on Sunday*: 'It has been a hard campaign to get justice for Becky. When we finally got to court, I had to sit and listen to things no parent should ever have to hear. I never knew that Becky hung around on street corners or realised how long she had been selling her body. I didn't know, until I saw the graphics in court, how little of her remains we buried. I felt sick to the stomach hearing that her head and arms were missing.

'I also had to watch Halliwell try and defend himself against the indefensible. When he was found guilty, he smirked. But he is not smirking now. We are finally having the last laugh. Now I can change her death certificate to say she was strangled – and I can put the date of her murder on her headstone.

'Finally, I will not rest until I have cleared Steve Fulcher's name.'

Fulcher continued a robust campaign in his own defence. He told the *Daily Mail*: 'It's taken all this time for Becky's case to come to court. But forensic evidence that has been used to convict Halliwell was available back in 2011. Wiltshire Police chose not to pursue it. Instead, resources went into investigating me for years.'

He went on to tell of his battle with authorities within the police service.

'No one wants to go back to the old days where the police sometimes ran roughshod over the rules, but the pendulum has swung way too far in favour of the criminal,' he said. 'There is an obsession with procedure at the expense of the bigger picture. If I had followed procedure, then Sian and Becky's bodies may never have been found – yet it seems that's what senior authorities would've preferred. The public needs to know what the police won't do if their own daughter went missing. It is a scandal.'

He reflected on how British policing has changed. A career copper, he joined what was then Sussex Police in 1986, aged twenty-one. As he rose through the ranks, he gained a postgraduate diploma, then master's degrees in criminology. Joining the Wiltshire force in 2003, he presided over dozens of large investigations, gaining a wealth of experience.

When Sian O'Callaghan was reported missing by her boyfriend after leaving a nightclub in Swindon town centre in the small hours, the CCTV footage of her getting into a taxi and the pinpointing of the mobile signal told him that there was a 'crime in action'.

'When you have a body in a ditch, you have a reactive investigation as the harm has been done,' he said. 'When you suspect someone has been abducted or kidnapped, their life remains under threat, and there are very clear procedural rules about that.'

The police *Kidnap Manual* gave precise guidelines.

'What that manual makes very clear is the primary crucial objective is the preservation of life,' said Fulcher. This places huge pressure on senior officers.

'It is a colossal effort. You are talking about co-ordinating hundreds of officers. You don't sleep, you don't eat, it's a 24/7 commitment,' added Fulcher. 'It's a race against time.'

There were emotions involved, too.

'I met Sian's parents and promised them I wouldn't rest until I found her,' he recalled.

His concern was for the victim and their family.

'That is always in your mind,' he said. 'They are someone's daughter, sister.'

Then a suspect came into view in the shape of taxi driver Christopher Halliwell, whose green Toyota Avensis had been seen near the nightclub and close to Savernake Forest, where the last signal from Sian's mobile had been located.

Covert surveillance was authorised in the hope that he would lead them to her. The police followed him as he took a fare to Heathrow Airport and down country lanes at night. They watched as a perfume bottle and bloody tissues were dumped in bins in remote rural areas, and the seat covers were dumped at a carwash. When Halliwell was spotted buying enough paracetamol to kill himself, Fulcher found he had no choice but to arrest him on suspicion of kidnap. This, too, presented him with a dilemma.

'It was a terrible catch 22. By effectively acting to ensure Halliwell's life was preserved, I was potentially going to cause the death of his victim,' he recalled. 'If Sian was still alive, she probably wouldn't survive the ninety-six hours we could keep him in custody if he refused to co-operate.'

Fulcher had paced the floor of the operations room as his men closed in.

As Halliwell was clearly suicide risk, Fulcher arranged an interview team to conduct a 'safety interview', under caution, at the scene of his arrest. But when Halliwell kept answering 'no comment', Fulcher made another crucial decision.

By then, the search for Sian centred round nearby Barbary Castle. So he authorised officers to bring Halliwell to the hilltop site alone for an 'urgent interview', which again was permissible under the *Manual*'s code. It was a last-ditch attempt to find Sian.

'I pleaded with him for Sian's life,' Fulcher said. For nine long minutes Halliwell parried questions. 'Then he said "Have you got a car, let's go." It was horribly tense. All I could do was try to keep him talking.'

Fulcher said he knew he was sailing close to the wind, but 'I wasn't hanging him over a motorway bridge to get a confession.'

Halliwell guided the police to an isolated lane where he said Sian's body was lying in the open. At this point, it changed from a kidnap into a murder case, subject to guidelines drawn up in the Police and Criminal Evidence Act of 1984, and Fulcher should have cautioned Halliwell again. However, Sian's body was not evident at first.

As Fulcher pointed out, however, his focus was on one thing – finding Sian. But, as forensic officers set to work, Fulcher was unprepared for what came next. While no body had been found, he could not be a hundred per cent sure she was dead. Perhaps she was still alive somewhere. His primary aim was to find her, and the only person who could help him was Halliwell.

'I gave him a cigarette and he asked to talk to me. It was a bonding moment,' Fulcher said. 'Success or failure hung on that moment. Any intervention could have broken it. We were puffing away on cigarettes and he was giving me information. If I had suddenly reminded him he had the right to remain silent, what would he have done?'

And the move paid off.

'We walked away and he said, "Do you want another one?" He then told me he had killed a girl in 2003, −4 or −5, and he could take me to that body – the exact spot.'

Again, this was a murder case and, under PACE guidelines, Fulcher should have cautioned Halliwell once more. Doing so, Fulcher maintained, would have meant losing the momentum. Halliwell would have had to be taken to a police station, where he would have been given a solicitor whose role was to stop clients incriminating themselves, and the chance of finding the dead girl's body would have been lost.

'You can criticise me, but I felt I had no option,' said Fulcher. 'There was simply no other way I could have acted that was within the letter of the law. There wasn't an alternative that wouldn't involve ruining my chances of Halliwell opening up.'

Fulcher was an experience cop making a judgment call. They got back into the car and Halliwell directed them to rural Gloucestershire.

'He was crying in the car, saying he was a sick f★★★er,' Fulcher recalled. 'He was scrolling through pictures on his phone of other women, leading me to suspect there were other victims. I was desperately trying to keep the lines of communication open, wondering how much else he might tell me.'

Once in the remote woodland, Halliwell stood on the exact spot where he claimed he had buried a girl years earlier. That girl was Becky Godden. Halliwell was then taken to the police station, where he was cautioned and, as Fulcher predicted, clammed up, refusing to answer any further questions.

Fulcher was congratulated by his superiors at the time. However, they showed little interest in pursuing charges relating to Becky Godden's murder, or looking for other victims.

'It seemed astonishing to me they were not pursuing lines of enquiry,' he said. 'Here was a man who indicated he might have more victims. Yet no one was interested.'

Fulcher asked to be transferred to the National Homicide Team. Then Halliwell's defence lawyers began their move to get the charges thrown out because Fulcher had not followed the PACE guidelines.

'I was prepared for this,' said Fulcher. 'His case wasn't defendable, so it was the only thing they could do – but I thought reason would prevail. I acted in good faith to save a life and to recover a body we did not previously know about.'

But Mrs Justice Cox ruled that Halliwell's confession was inadmissible. Meanwhile, Wiltshire Police failed to gather other evidence in the Becky Godden case.

'The CPS [Crown Prosecution Service] and senior police figures panicked,' said Fulcher. 'The CPS should have appealed. Instead, everyone turned on me.'

Then his conduct was referred to the Independent Police Complaints Commission.

'I offered to give them full and frank disclosure immediately. I heard nothing for ten months.'

Meanwhile, he was suspended and left pacing the floor at

home in frustration. This turned to serious concern when he learned the CPS were considering bringing charges against him for malfeasance in public office.

'I couldn't believe it,' he said. 'This is a charge that usually applies to corrupt officials, not someone dealing with a serial killer.'

Becky's mother, Karen Edwards, accompanied Fulcher to IPCC hearings to show her support. It did little good. In January 2014, he was found guilty of gross misconduct and given a severe reprimand. Though he kept his job, he soon felt he no choice but to resign.

"There had been years of endless worry as they investigated me,' he said. 'I felt my position was untenable.'

His family stuck by him, but shared his suffering.

'It has been devastating for everyone,' he said.

Two more years went by before Fulcher received his vindication when the trial judge, Sir John Griffith Williams, told Halliwell: 'But for your confession, I have no doubt Becky's remains would never have been found. You then tried to manipulate the police and court process to try to avoid getting what you deserved.'

A weight was lifted from his shoulders.

'The judge said I acted in good faith,' he said. "There is a fundamental flaw in the law when a detective has to refuse a voluntary confession from a suspect.'

Wiltshire Police had wasted valuable effort in a crusade against an officer for failing to follow procedure. But in retrospect, Fulcher found none of that surprising. He told the *Mail*: 'The senior echelons aren't police officers at all. Most aren't concerned with policing on the ground, but are pen-pushers.'

Not that he advocated breaking the rules.

'PACE is there for a reason,' he said. 'Quite rightly it gives protection to the innocent. But without common sense it gives too much protection to the guilty and not the victim. And if we're not protecting the victim then we're all sunk.'

Despite the fact that no evidence has been discovered to link Halliwell with other crimes and he has not been interviewed further, Fulcher believes that there were other victims.

'There's no question in my mind Halliwell murdered other girls,' he said. 'I made that clear back in 2011. There's no question, from all the information I gathered when I was running this inquiry in 2011, that he has committed other murders.'

Meanwhile, the trail in these cases has gone increasingly cold. Fulcher told the *Today* programme on BBC Radio 4 on 26 September 2016: 'I spent a lot of time with Christopher Halliwell. He was contrite, fully contrite, crying on my shoulder when I dealt with him. There's no question, from all the information I gathered when I was running this inquiry in 2011, that he has committed other murders. There's lots of things, but the principal thing he said was "The police want to interview me about eight murders."'

Asked whether he felt he had been hung out to dry, Fulcher said: 'I have, obviously.'

Experts believe that there could have been earlier killings. Most serial killers begin their 'careers' in the late teens or early twenties. They do not suddenly start killing when they reach middle age. According to cellmate Ernest Springer, Halliwell even admitted an earlier murder. Springer told the *Daily Mail*: 'He told me that he had been having sex with a woman and she asked him to strangle her, not to kill her, but for a thrill. He said: "So I did. I strangled her so she would not be having sex with anyone else."

'I asked him a few days later if he'd actually killed her, but he got very aggressive. He was rolling a fag and knocked his tobacco tin off the table, saying: "I don't want to talk about it."'

Experts also thought waiting eight years between a first and a second victim did not fit the pattern of serial killers. But those people who tried to link Halliwell to two, possibly three, notorious unsolved cases – Sally Ann John in 1995, Linda Razzell in 2002 and Claudia Lawrence in 2009 – were merely speculating.

Karen Edwards was disappointed that no grounds were found for the police to investigate possible links and angry that dossiers Fulcher created in 2011 about Halliwell's vehicles and associations were never distributed to the forty-three police forces across the country.

'They were meant to have been distributed to other police but were never given out,' she told the *Mail on Sunday*. 'That is the real miscarriage of justice.'

Steve Fulcher revealed that a stash of puzzling pencil drawings was seized at Halliwell's home. 'There were a good dozen or so sketches that I saw and they were all of remote locations. One of my lines of inquiry was obviously to try to identify where these places were,' said Fulcher. 'The theory I was working on was that if I could find those locations I could find other victims.'

He called in experts to help identify the locations and supplied sketches to other police forces. 'I wanted as many people as possible trying to identify these places,' he said. 'I left the inquiry a few weeks after and I don't know what happened after that.'

Recalling Halliwell's sketches, he added: 'They struck me as an odd choice of subject for an amateur artist.' He learned from a psychologist that 'things like sketches could be sexual triggers subsequently. So he would look at a scene he has drawn and recall a victim and that would engender a sexual response.'

From his prison cell, Halliwell sent sick letters mocking his conviction for murdering Becky Godden. Insisting he was innocent of her murder, Halliwell complained: 'Short of the deceased walking into court and sitting on the judge's lap, I was going to be found guilty whatever happened.'

He defended his handling of the case.

'I went into court to tell it like it was and it was important to me that whatever I had to say came from me, not a lawyer,' he said. 'And yes, I laughed at a guilty verdict. I found it ironic that I was found guilty of killing someone I've never met. But I do deserve the previous life sentence for Sian's death. I had no right to lose my temper the way I did.'

He also wrote of his animosity to Steve Fulcher.

'While he was in the witness box I said to him that it was a pleasure ruining his career and I called him a corrupt bastard,' he said. 'I've got no regrets on that point. His one and only mistake was he threatened my kids and he's paying for it.'

The whole process had been a pain. He moaned: 'The last six months have been a headache, having trawled through 11,000 pages of documents with little sleep. I've no regrets, I told the truth and it didn't go down well. It is what it is. I don't know if I'll appeal. I certainly have plenty of grounds for it, but at the moment I'm spent and haven't got the will for another fight. Not yet.'

CLEARING THE DETECTIVE'S NAME

In prison letters, Halliwell told of how he earned £17 a week behind bars, which keeps him in tobacco and coffee. He also talked of his hobbies, including restoring classic cars, which are 'irrelevant now'.

'In 2007/8/9, I restored a canal barge which I intended to live on but I sold it to pay off debts after my divorce,' he said. 'And I used to restore classic cars, one of which is in a museum. I never drank because I never knew when I might have to use my car. A phone call from a customer could come at any hour and I had to be sober.'

Halliwell also said he got letters from autograph hunters. In one letter he begged for a photo. It was from his pen pal, known only as Melissa. In his reply, he rued that serving life as a heterosexual meant he would never have another sexual partner.

'I like your description of yourself,' he wrote to Melissa. 'A photo in the future would be better. Your letter seemed genuine and you now have my curious side thinking! I laughed when you wrote you might remain single for a while. Yep, same as. I'm not gay – so it's guaranteed I'll be single until I croak!'

Halliwell's admission that he deserved his life sentence for killing Sian was of little comfort to her mother, Elaine.

'Sometimes, when I know everyone in the house has gone to sleep, I let my mind wander back to that night,' she told *The Sun*. 'I wonder what her final moments were like. Who did she cry out for? But then I pull myself back together and try my best to get on with it.'

Becky's murder trial bought memories of her dead daughter back.

'Sian was such a bubbly, happy girl,' she remembered.

'Always dancing around to Craig David and Michael Jackson. She tried college after her GCSEs, but it wasn't for her, so she got a job in admin and really enjoyed it. She was a doting sister, too, and like a second mother to her youngest brother Aiden. I'd often wake up in the morning to find him sleeping in her bed. I know she would have been a fantastic mother.'

The last time she saw her eldest alive was two weeks before her murder.

'Sian had moved out of home in January 2011 with her boyfriend Kevin Reape, then twenty-five. That night she came over and it was just the two of us,' remembers Elaine. 'I made her favourite meal – lamb with mint sauce.'

When they kissed goodbye, Elaine had no idea she would never see her daughter again.

Since the death of her beloved daughter, Elaine had been working with the Suzy Lamplugh Trust and Child Bereavement UK.

'Something good has to come from all this,' she said.

Slowly the family were coming to terms with the loss of Sian.

'We're now trying to remember how she was instead of what happened to her,' she said. 'We're getting to the point where we want to include her in our conversations and laugh about times with her. As hard as that is, we want to be able to do that. Sian deserves that much. I'm not consumed with anger. Sian wouldn't want that.'

CHAPTER TWENTY-TWO

SALLY ANN JOHN

Sally Ann John was twenty-three when she disappeared on 8 September 1995, but despite continuous appeals she has never been heard of again. She was last seen on a Friday night in the Swindon's Manchester Road red light district. Despite a major missing persons inquiry over the following three months, no trace of her was found. However, following a cold-case review, Wiltshire Police launched a murder investigation in November 2014.

The police revisited witnesses, and the family and friends of Sally.

'This reinvestigation was initiated following a review of the original investigation and significant new lines of inquiry were established,' said Detective Inspector Tim Corner. 'This has been reclassified as a murder investigation as detectives believe it is likely that Sally was murdered following her disappearance in 1995.'

THE GRINNING KILLER

New appeal posters were distributed in the area and others places familiar to Sally Ann, who was working as a prostitute at the time of her death. The poster carried two pictures of Sally Ann, and read:

MURDER
Disappearance of Sally Ann John in 1995
Police are appealing for any information regarding what they now believe was the murder of Sally Ann John, aged twenty-three, in 1995.

Sally went missing on 8 September 1995 from the Station Road/Aylesbury Street area in Swindon.

Last year, detectives declared this a murder investigation.

- Did you know Sally Ann John in 1995?
- Do you have information that you didn't give to the police?
- Did you see Sally Ann in September and see who she was with?
- Do you have any information about the person responsible?

If you have any information please contact Wilshire Police on
101
Or Crimestoppers anonymous on
0800 555 111
www.wiltshire.police.uk

Sally was born and bred in Swindon and lived at the time in the Nythe. She was close to her family and friends and especially to her mother, Lesley. The last confirmed sighting of Sally was at 10.45 p.m. around Aylesbury Street and Station Road. She was wearing a short, pink, nightie-style dress, a black jacket, black shoes and black thigh-length socks.

During the initial investigation, fellow sex workers and her boyfriend were interviewed. Initially, it was thought they may have left Swindon voluntarily, but a search of her flat showed that she had not taken any clothes or her mobile phone.

The flat was only yards away from where Halliwell lived when he was first married in the mid-1990s.

When Halliwell was arrested for the murder of Sian O'Callaghan in 2011, Sally Ann's father, Glyn John, contacted Wiltshire Police.

'I went to the police and told them Sally Ann would have been known to Halliwell,' he said.

At that stage, Sally Ann, who had worked at the Swindon head office of the Triumph International lingerie company before getting involved with drugs and prostitution, and was still classified as a missing person.

An old friend said: 'She was a very nice girl, and it was a shame she got into the bad company she did. She used to go to school with my sister and would come to our house all the time, and it was dreadful how things turned out for her. I have always been wondering what happened to her, just like everyone else has been. It is quite encouraging to hear they are looking back into this, and I just hope that something is found so that this can bring her family a bit of closure.'

Sally Ann's murder investigation ran alongside further enquiries being made into activities of Halliwell in Operation Manilla

'This investigation is in no way linked with any other

murder enquiries and it would be inappropriate for me to comment on the ongoing Operation Manilla because the two investigations are not connected,' said DI Corner. 'I met with Sally's parents and informed them that this is being reinvestigated and they welcomed the reinvestigation. The John family need closure into the disappearance of their daughter. There can be nothing worse for a parent than to lose a daughter under these circumstances and not know what has actually happened to them.'

After Halliwell was charged with Becky Godden's murder, Sally Ann's mother, Lesley, appealed for information on television.

'My daughter was a bright and beautiful girl who could make anyone smile,' she said tearfully. 'Someone out there knows what happened to Sally... I would urge them to come forward – they may not have spoken to police at the time she disappeared but now they might be able to. That small bit of information might be the key to giving us closure and finally knowing what happened to our girl. It won't bring her back but it will ease our suffering. Please help us find her.'

Six months later, the police spent a week searching Sally Ann's last known address in Kimmeridge Close, in the Nythe area of Swindon. They used ground-penetrating radar and 'blood dogs' from South Wales.

'Items of note have been discovered and we are currently considering the best course with regards to runner examination,' said a police spokesman.

DCI Jeremy Carter added: 'The search in this location has been completed and I am now taking expert advice on what runner examination is required of several items found. This may have been a "cold case" but forensic technology and investigative policing has moved on dramatically and I will ensure that we use every possible tool available to us to identify those responsible for Sally Ann's death. The search at this location may have ended but we are following a number of new lines of enquiry and I am positive that we are now closer to discovering the truth.

'I would like to reiterate our thanks to the occupants of the house who have no involvement in this investigation, and the local community for their assistance and co-operation.'

Soon after, three men in their fifties from Swindon and Chippenham were arrested. Halliwell was not one of them. All three were released on bail.

DCI Carter said, 'I am fully aware of the Halliwell case. While I am keeping an open mind we are not making links with that matter at this time.'

Even though no evidence had been found linking Halliwell to the murder of Sally Ann, Fulcher was suspicious.

'She was a prostitute from Broad Street in Swindon, where Halliwell lived,' he said. 'He is known to have had a relationship with Sally Ann.'

Karen Edwards agreed.

'She was a Swindon girl and knew him well,' she said. 'She used to live in the same street as Halliwell, babysit his kids and take his taxis.'

Halliwell not only accepted fares from so-called working girls, he has also admitted using them and having one-night stands with female passengers. He told the police that he had used the services of prostitutes 'seven or eight times' but added: 'I never went with the same girl twice.'

However, there remains no evidence implicating Halliwell.

CHAPTER TWENTY-THREE

LINDA RAZZELL

On the morning of 19 March 2002, forty-one-year-old Linda Razzell left her home in Highworth, near Swindon, with her four children and her boyfriend. She dropped the children at school and took her partner to work before parking in Alvescot Road and walking towards Swindon College, where she worked as a learning-support assistant.

Linda was never seen again. She was reported missing after she failed to pick up her two youngest children from an after-school club. The police suspected that she had been abducted after her mobile phone was found near her abandoned car.

Two months later, they arrested her estranged husband, Glyn Razzell, a forty-four-year-old unemployed former investment banker. Their marriage had fallen apart in 1998, after Linda confessed to an affair with a builder working at their home.

Spots of blood eventually found in the Renault Laguna Glyn Razzell had borrowed matched Linda's, though two earlier forensic examinations had failed to find them. His motive for killing her, the prosecution said, was to avoid a crippling divorce settlement.

Razzell's defence team maintain that the incriminating blood was discovered only after a third forensic examination and was deliberately planted. They also said there was no blood, hair or fibres connected with his wife on his clothing and no sign that any blood or other evidence had been washed away. Glyn Razzell was convicted of her murder in 2003 and jailed for life. In 2008, the Criminal Cases Review Commission decided against referring the case to the Court of Appeal.

During his long years in prison, Glyn Razzell has continued to protest his innocence. His solicitor, Rob Ross, does not believe that he did it. Nor does his sister, Vicky George, who led the Justice For Glyn Razzell campaign and runs its website. Nor does Becky Godden's mother, Karen Edwards, who compiled a dossier on the case.

Halliwell certainly worked as a builder, it emerged at his trial. He drifted from job to job, including spells working as a window cleaner and as a ground worker in the building trade. In 1996, shortly after the Razzells bought the house, they were granted planning permission by Swindon Borough Council for a two-storey extension to accommodate their growing family. In court, Glyn Razzell said the breakdown of his marriage 'was caused principally by Linda's infidelity with builders who were adding an extension on [their] house in 1998'.

Her initially missing mobile phone was later found hidden under a piece of wood in an alleyway off Swindon's Drove

Road, where the police believed that Linda had been seized.

Phone records show that Glyn Razzell took a call on his home landline at 8.24 that morning. His supporters insist he could not have hung up, got in his car and driven to the alleyway, on a busy school route, in time to stage an abduction.

CCTV did not show the Renault Laguna Razzell used in the area that day, while experts have accounted for every mile the car was driven. Razzell said he was walking past the city's Westlea police station at the time Linda was believed to have been abducted, but the CCTV cameras there were not working.

'I don't think anyone in their right mind would have claimed they'd walked past a police station if they hadn't,' said his solicitor, Rob Ross. 'I got to know him exceptionally well and I still find it difficult to believe that the man I got to know could have done what he was alleged to have done.'

Ross believes Linda, who suffered from depression, ran away after clearing her bank accounts the day before. Police twice searched Razzell's car, along with sink traps at his home, and found nothing incriminating. It was only after a third examination of the Renault a week later, using a different forensic technique, that minute spots of blood matching Linda's were found in the boot and under the parcel shelf. There was no other evidence linking Glyn Razzell to Linda's disappearance.

Ross said the blood 'was always going to be a problem, because we could not find an explanation as to why it was there'.

'The information that has come to light following the conviction of Halliwell for the murder of Becky Godden requires our careful consideration,' said a new post on the

Justice for Glyn Razzell website. 'We acknowledge the huge significance this has for Glyn in his fight to clear his name.

Steve Fulcher agreed, drawing attention to the parallels between Linda's disappearance and Sian's murder.

'Linda is thought to have had a relationship with her builder,' he said. 'Halliwell did building work at her house. She has been missing since March 19, 2002, and there are potential issues with the forensics in the investigation.'

'At the time of the Razzell case, no one mentioned Christopher Halliwell,' said Ross. 'If there is a link to Linda, then of course it should be investigated.'

After Halliwell was convicted for the murder of Becky Godden, Vicky George drove from her home in Essex to the Category C Guys Marsh Prison in Dorset, where she told Razzell about the possibility that Halliwell might be Linda's killer.

'When I told Glyn he broke down and cried, saying, "I always thought we would find Linda alive,"' she said. He had clung to the hope that his wife had secretly fled abroad to start a new life after their split.

A spokesman for his family said: 'It is imperative Wiltshire Police properly investigate any links between Halliwell and Linda.'

But Linda's family maintained the right man was already behind bars. They had 'no doubt' her husband was guilty. A spokesman told BBC Wales: 'We were a hundred per cent happy with the police investigation. There is no doubt in our minds who the murderer was. There is no validity in the detective's claim.'

Linda's boyfriend, Greg Worrall, who was living with her at the time of her disappearance, said: 'There's no link between Halliwell and Glyn Razzell. Razzell should stay in prison for the rest of his life, he's shown no remorse. He knows exactly where Linda's body is. One day he will show some remorse and lead us to her body and we can finally have a proper funeral. Razzell is just using the situation. Swindon's a big place. Is there only one murderer in Swindon?'

But Fulcher was concerned that there had not been a wider investigation.

'We know that Halliwell has killed women, has a propensity for killing women, and had a direct relationship with Linda Razzell. Whether or not he's responsible isn't the issue. The issue is why no investigation has occurred.'

However, Glyn Razell was convicted of his wife's murder and there remains no evidence linking Halliwell to her disappearance.

CHAPTER TWENTY-FOUR

CLAUDIA
LAWRENCE

The last sighting of Claudia Lawrence, the thirty-five-year-old daughter of a Yorkshire solicitor, was on CCTV on 18 March 2009, when she could be seen strolling across Melrosegate Bridge after leaving work at University of York's Goodricke College, where she was a chef.

That evening, she phoned her mother to make plans for the forthcoming Mothering Sunday, and sent and received texts. She was reported missing when she failed to turn up for work at the university on 19 March – the day both Sian O'Callaghan and Linda Razzell went missing.

The investigation into her disappearance was reclassified from a missing person's case to a murder inquiry six weeks later. Back in 2009, one of the key police appeals was to identify a left-handed man who was seen smoking on Melrosegate Bridge at around the time Claudia was there. He was slim and thought to be around five foot six inches tall. Halliwell was a little taller, at five foot eight to ten inches, but was slim, left-handed and smoked. Four men were arrested on suspicion of her murder after raids in March and April 2016 but none faced charges. Halliwell was not a suspect.

'Claudia Lawrence disappeared from York seven years ago,' said Fulcher after the Becky Godden trial. 'It fits his pattern of behaviour – abducting women walking alone either late at night or early in the morning.' But no evidence linking Halliwell with the disappearance of Claudia Lawrence has been found.

Karen Edwards, who had good reason to study multiple murderers, added her voice to those accusing Halliwell of other slayings.

'He is definitely a serial killer. I believe he has been up and down the country murdering young women,' she told the *Mail on Sunday*. 'He used to be a ground worker up north – I know somebody who worked with him on the same building site. He would go and have a pint with the lads and then disappear. Serial killers are usually triggered by dates. That was the day that Halliwell broke up with one of his partners. Halliwell was familiar with York – his father lived in Huddersfield – and the description of Claudia's murderer is identical to him – a left-handed smoker, five foot eight to ten inches, with slightly receding hair and a skinny build. Claudia was reported missing from her home on 19 March 2009 – exactly two years to the day before Sian, the same date that Linda Razzell disappeared.'

While Halliwell lived in Swindon, his job as a chauffeur and taxi driver would have taken him all over the country. Karen also drew the comparison between Halliwell and American serial killer Ted Bundy, who murdered more than thirty people.

'Halliwell represented himself like Ted Bundy and I only hope that if he killed as many people as Bundy, we find out sooner rather than later,' she said.

As well as believing Halliwell had killed other women, she also had grounds to believe that he had raped and beaten many more.

'During my campaigning, I uncovered numerous stories which I passed on to the police of girls who had lucky escapes in the back of his taxi,' she said. 'He drove one girl who got into his taxi, to a wooded area, which terrified her and she screamed. It was only after he was disturbed that he drove her back to Swindon. Quite a lot of the people I encountered have given statements to the police, so hopefully Halliwell will face more charges.'

Karen said her fight was for the families of other missing women, whose bodies lie in shallow, unmarked graves.

Reacting to Steve Fulcher's remarks, North Yorkshire Police said: 'The investigation team is aware of this matter and they will carefully assess the information in line with the ongoing review of the Claudia Lawrence case. However, to be clear, the team is not aware of any evidence that would link this individual to the disappearance and suspected murder of Claudia.' Simply put, Halliwell is not a suspect.

Claudia's seventy-two-year-old mother, Joan, said: 'I've never given up hope Claudia may still be alive,' and urged North Yorkshire Police to reactivate their investigation.

'It is a line of inquiry the police can't ignore,' she said. 'They need to know where Halliwell was on March 18 and 19. Was he in Yorkshire on those days, or did he have an alibi?'

Claudia's seventy-year-old father, Peter, said: 'North Yorkshire Police obviously need to take this seriously and see if there is anything to it. We have been through this so many times over the past seven years. Similar things happening and you just want it to be either found to be true and then it can be put to bed, or found not to be true and then we can forget it.'

However, he said he was surprised that Fulcher had spoken out to the press, and urged him to give all the information he had to North Yorkshire Police.

'He knows the score and procedure,' said Peter Lawrence. 'It's far more important to go and talk to North Yorkshire Police than talk to the press. That's not where you go to. It's been a rollercoaster all the time for the family, and the rest of the family will have woken up this morning to see this all in the papers. I'm surprised the way it's come out.'

Wiltshire Police now accept Halliwell was probably a serial killer. Cold-case expert Chris Clark, who has supplied leads to the force on other cases, believed the Lawrence case involved Halliwell: 'I believe he had the method, motive and opportunity.'

Wiltshire Police Chief Constable Mike Veale said, however, that the force had not uncovered any links between Halliwell and other murders 'at this time'.

He said: 'As a result of the obvious emotions and complexities of this case, the public criticism and unjustified challenge of Wiltshire Police was entirely predicted and expected, but the force made the ethical decision to maintain its position of not rising to the sensational and unsubstantiated claims and speculation. We did this because we believed these sorts of claims would create a media frenzy and in turn lead to the families of people who have gone missing or tragically been murdered being re-traumatised and put into impossible positions.

'Their expectations, their feelings and their distress would be unnecessarily dragged once again into the media spotlight. This is something which I believe is unforgivable, injudicious and insensitive. This was reinforced to me when I spoke to the mothers of some of those named during the coverage of this case, who told me they had been traumatised and distressed by this unfounded speculation involving their loved ones.'

Meanwhile, a spokesman for North Yorkshire Police spoke out over the unhelpful speculation regarding the Claudia Lawrence case.

'North Yorkshire Police's Major Crime Unit has shared information with the investigation team from Wiltshire Police, which established that Halliwell's father was not a resident of York or the North Yorkshire area, as had been suggested. He also passed away in 1992,' the spokesman said. 'It can be confirmed that on the information provided by Wiltshire Police, there are no known links between Halliwell and the Claudia Lawrence case. The senior investigating officer in the Claudia Lawrence investigation has been in contact with both Joan and Peter Lawrence following last weekend's speculation of these links, particularly that Halliwell's father lived around the corner. This type of speculation does not help the family.'

Fulcher added: 'I am going to be taking this through the political process, through my MP Sir Nicholas Soames. I'm not able to go into further detail but I'm asking for an inquiry into the failure of Wiltshire Police to investigate. I shall be asking for it at the most senior level of government.'

Martin Dales, a spokesman for the Lawrence family, told of their distress.

'It has been an ongoing nightmare, particularly for parents Joan and Peter and sister Ali, as they wait for news of her whereabouts,' he said. 'I know North Yorkshire Police have worked tirelessly to find the answer, but it is high time whoever is responsible for Claudia's disappearance came clean. How can someone be so cruel for this length of time? I think the retired officer in question has a detailed knowledge of things. The overriding point is really, whoever has done whatever to Claudia, it has been an incredibly long time. It's a heartbreaking period to go without somebody and we hope this will come to some conclusion – whether this is it is for other people to find out. There are pluses and minuses of thinking: "Are we going to get some sort of conclusion or is this just another false dawn?" All the time, Claudia is still not here. It's got to be thoroughly checked out.'

CHAPTER TWENTY-FIVE

MELANIE HALL

The murders of Sian O'Callaghan and Becky Godden brought fresh anguish to the family of Melanie Hall, who was twenty-five when she disappeared in 1996 in similar circumstances. The psychology graduate was a clerical officer in the orthopaedic department at Bath's Royal United Hospital when she went to the Cadillacs nightclub with her boyfriend, Philip Karlbaum, a German doctor she had met at the hospital, and a group of friends. The couple had a row when he saw her dancing with another man. She was last seen sitting on a stool near the dance floor at 1 a.m. on 9 June.

Avon and Somerset Police questioned clubbers and local taxi drivers, but her fate remained a mystery for thirteen years until her remains were found hidden under five plastic bin bags at the side of the M5 in Gloucestershire in October 2009 by a workman clearing undergrowth along the slip road at junction 14, north of Bristol. She was initially identified by a ring she was wearing that had been in her family for generations; this was confirmed by dental records. The discovery came after police had searched the River Avon several times, quizzed thousands of clubbers and taxi drivers, and appealed for information on TV's *Crimewatch*, all without success.

A thousand mourners turned up at Melanie's funeral at Bath Abbey in December 2009. Her father, Steve Hall, a former chairman of Bath City FC, spoke of the torment he and his wife were suffering.

'It has caused untold anguish for my wife, myself and my family, an anguish that will not go away over the years to come,' he said. 'People out there know, they've lived with that secret. Now I'm appealing for the person who knows to come forward. We had a young vibrant daughter with a bright future in front of her. Today we have a bag of bones discarded here on the side of a motorway.'

Melanie's mother Pat added: 'I feel very angry that her body has been dumped on the road like a sack of garbage.'

Fulcher remarked on similarities between the murders of Sian and Becky and that of Melanie Hall.

Bath is a short drive along the motorway from Swindon. Both Sian and Becky were petite, like Melanie, and all three disappeared after leaving a nightclub. Melanie had been battered to death and her skull was fractured. Sian also died from head injuries. It is not known how Becky died, though her head was missing.

Avon and Somerset Police also said that Halliwell was the strongest suspect yet for the murder of Melanie Hall. Her remains were found tied together with a piece of blue rope. Halliwell's internet-browsing history revealed he heavily researched rope knots and binding techniques.

Over the years, a number of suspects have been arrested, but none were charged. In September 1998, officers visited Durham Prison to interview notorious sex killer John Cannan. He was in jail at the time Melanie went missing, but police believed his former cellmate, convicted rapist Christopher Clark, could have been involved. Known as the 'early bird rapist' for a string of knife-point sex attacks on women in the 1980s, Clark was jailed for life in 1997 for pulling a plastic bag over a twenty-three-year-old teacher's head and indecently assaulting her yards from a bail hostel in Bath where he was being held on probation. No charges in relation to Melanie Hall were brought.

The police also questioned convicted sex killer Marc Shillibier, who was already serving life for the vicious 1999 murder of eighteen-year-old Rebecca Storrs, when she spurned his advances. She was smashed over the head with a hammer. Her mutilated body was found in a river seven hours later. 'I killed her,' he confessed to a friend. 'She was still breathing when I left her. I don't know why. I gutted her like a fish.'

Shillibier had also stood trial in 1998 for the murder of a forty-five-year-old gay man who, it was claimed, he had picked up for sex and later stabbed and set alight. While he was acquitted, the police made it clear they were not looking for anyone else in connection with the crime. He later allegedly told a cellmate that he had murdered Melanie Hall, but withdrew his claim and refused to co-operate with detectives. Melanie's body had also been burned after her murder. Again, no charges were brought.

Then, in January 2016, Levi Bellfield, who raped and murdered Milly Dowler and others, confessed in jail. But any link to the murder of Melanie Hall was dismissed and her parents concluded that he was just playing games.

The police have not ruled out links between the murder of Melanie Hall and that of Suzy Lamplugh, the twenty-five-year-old estate agent who went missing in Fulham, south-west London in July 1986, and whose body has never been found. Another suspect was a serial sex attacker in Bath, nicknamed the 'Batman rapist' after he left a baseball cap bearing a Batman logo at the scene of one attack. Then there was the unknown assailant who threatened to slit a woman's throat and slashed her hand as he tried to force her into a car a few hundred yards from Cadillacs just hours before Melanie was abducted.

In June 2016, Melanie's parents Pat and Steve offered their £50,000 life savings for information about the murder of their daughter. *The Sun* matched the sum, bumping up the reward to £100,000. The Halls were then in their seventies and wanted to see justice done for their daughter before they died.

Retired builder and lecturer Steve told the newspaper: 'We have a crusade in Melanie's name and we are giving up money originally set aside to help us in old age. We'd rather die poor than not know who killed Melanie. We want to see this through before we pop our clogs. It marks the last thing we can physically do on behalf of Melanie as her parents.'

Former nurse Pat wept, saying: 'The only thing we can do is hope to find who it was who did what they did to her. To be left by the side of the road for thirteen years in a bin bag with no clothes. You wouldn't do that to your dog.'

The Sun also ran 'A Personal Plea by Mel's Dad'. It read:

I'm appealing personally to someone out there who knows what has happened to my daughter Melanie.

Whoever that person is, you and I have a bond between us.

I have the terrible agony of having lost a daughter, brutally murdered on the streets of Bath, you know what has happened or know the people who have been involved in Melanie's demise. I want to share with you my agony in a way that is positive and that will help you and will help me. If you come forward with the information that will help me find the killer of my daughter, I in return want to help you reshape your life with a financial reward. In association with the *Sun* newspaper we're looking at a sum of £100,000. That is a lot of money that can change your life for the better and that will happen if you help me with information. So I appeal to you to come forward and tell me what you know about the demise of my daughter and I will help you shape your life for the future.

After Halliwell was convicted of Becky Godden's murder, Fulcher said: 'The circumstances match his modus operandi in abducting a girl, late at night, from a nightclub. Evidence of her being tied up with rope is consistent with Halliwell's interests.'

Karen Edwards added: 'She was taken by an unmarked taxi.'

Once again, however, there remains no evidence linking Halliwell with the murder of Melanie Hall.

CHAPTER TWENTY-SIX

MISSING WOMEN

Other names of missing women came up in the investigation. One was that of Thi Hai Nguyen, who was just twenty years old when she went missing from her lodgings in Swindon in October 2005. She had arrived in the UK in 2003 and was living in Hesketh Crescent, not far from Suju nightclub.

She was five foot two inches tall, slim, with shoulder-length black hair streaked with blonde and the police thought she may have gone to London to find work. When the second body that Halliwell had led the police to was eventually found, it was initially thought to be Thi Hai Nguyen, before it was identified as Becky Godden. Thi Hai Nguyen has still not been found.

Thirty-nine-year-old Tina Pryer was tipped as Wiltshire's 'one outstanding' missing person before the second body was identified as that of Becky Godden. A cleaner at the University of Bath and a local primary school, she lived with her estranged partner and three young children, then aged between six and ten. She told her children she was going to London for a while, and was last seen getting into a taxi at her home in Trowbridge in 2001. Appealing for help, her sister, Dawn Curtis, said she could not understand why Tina had not contacted her children since she disappeared.

Mrs Curtis said at the time Miss Pryer suffered from epilepsy and dyslexia and the family were worried about her safety. 'We just want to know she is still alive,' she said in July 2001.

At the time, police said they thought she had taken a train to London and did not believe she had come to any harm, although she never got back in touch with her family. The family dismissed any suggestion of a connection to Halliwell because Tina had been suffering from depression before her disappearance, while the *Western Daily Press* reported that she 'is now understood to have been later found safe and well in Weston-super-Mare'.

Then there was twenty-one-year-old Sandra Brewin, who disappeared from her parents', home in the Peatmoor suburb of Swindon in 1994. Her parents, John and Nora, think their daughter's problems began in June that year when she became penfriends with a man who was in prison in Oxfordshire. She remains on the list of missing persons.

Halliwell has been convicted on overwhelming evidence of two brutal murders of young women. He is now serving a whole-life sentence and will die in prison. Whatever speculation swirls around him, there is no evidence to date which would justify his arrest, interview and charge in relation to any other crime.